MW01132028

Praise for
BE-FRIEND YOURSELF

"*BE-Friend Yourself* is all about creating a relationship with food and body that's filled with warmth and goodness. This beautiful book is written with honesty, insight and love. Marla Mervis-Hartmann weaves together timeless wisdom, great storytelling, and sweet reflections on her own personal journey. You'll be inspired to make lasting changes when it comes to your body, and your life. And you'll learn how to create a new and healthier inner dialogue around food. If you're ready to dive deeper into yourself and see what's in the way of your happiness, then this book can help you finally find the freedom and peace that you truly deserve."

– **Marc David**: Founder of the Institute for the Psychology of Eating, and author of *Nourishing Wisdom* and *The Slow Down Diet*.

"Marla writes with such amazing honesty that she soon feels like your best friend! Marla's stories and those of her clients give real insight into the struggles of many who suffer from all types of eating disorders. If I could foretell the future, I'd predict this book will bring many to start their own path to recovery!"

– **Cathy Meyer-Uyehara**, FACHE, CEO, Ai Pono
(ED Recovery Center) in Hawaii

"I love this book! As a clinician working with survivors of trauma, and perhaps equally importantly as a survivor myself, this book is a gift. Written with love and a broad knowledge base, Marla provides real life, easy to understand tools for deep healing. For those of us who have ever experienced our bodies as an unhappy place to be, or food as a coping mechanism or a curse, this book is for you. Like talking to good friend, this is perfect model for how we can can talk with ourselves! HIGHLY recommended!"

– **Janet Farnsworth**, MSW, RYT, Body Empowerment & Intimacy Coach

"I love this book! Marla's words are a gentle guide to help you redefine your relationship with your body. She shows you how to befriend yourself ~ how to appreciate the beauty you are and how to move into an abiding state of healing. A much needed light in this world, Marla teaches us to be kind, and intuitive. She reminds us to trust ourself. She calls us back to self-love. This book is a message the world needs now more than ever.

Have you ever looked in the mirror and noticed who's looking at who? If you're like most people, you'll feel like the person in the mirror is looking at you — like the world is looking at you, causing you to question yourself and your appearance. But our life is not about who the world wants us to be. It's about allowing our authentic unconditioned self to shine. Marla Mervis Hartmann's new book, *BE-Friend Yourself*, is a beautiful story about rediscovering and loving ourselves exactly as we are. It's time for all of us to Be-Friend Ourselves. I love this book!"

— **Jacob Israel Liberman**, author of *Luminous Life: How the Science of Light Unlocks the Art of Living*

"Everyone knows diets don't work. Yet many don't know what does...until now. *BE-Friend Yourself: Finding Freedom with Food and Peace with Your Body* highlights the true path to healing and wholeness. Through personal, honest stories about herself and her clients, as well as step-by-step practices, Marla gently guides the reader back to herself—to her Authentic Power. This is the pot of gold waiting on the other side, that can never be taken away, for those ready to do the inner work."

— **Amber Krzys**, M.A. 1 founder, Fierce Loving, Inc.

"With entertaining and relatable anecdotes, Marla guides the reader from self-loathing to self-love and shares how this shift informs our food and exercise choices to improve overall health and well-being. This is a beautiful book for those who want to quiet their inner critic and feel good in their body, heal their relationship with food, and reclaim how powerful it is to be a woman."

— **Sharon Brock**, bestselling author of *The LOVEE Method: Mindfulness Meditation for Breast Cancer*

"As a man, I've denied I needed to read a book like this. I found my shadow relationship with food thoroughly revealed and then tenderly held with every page. Brilliant wisdom born out of authentic and vulnerable expose."

– **Jonathon Barbato**, CO-CEO Best Ever Channels &
Founder of the MORE U Channel

"I've been a witness to Marla's personal healing journey for over twenty years. In this book, Marla weaves her personal experience, professional expertise and along with client's stories into this powerful testimonial for non diet approach to food and body. The stories are intimate, empowering, raw and honest. Thankful to have women, like Marla, sharing this work with all women."

– **Kate Williams Stone**, Non-Diet Health and Life Coach
for Perimenopause

"*Be-Friend Yourself* is a beacon of positivity and self-love, resonating with women of all ages. Marla beautifully articulates the journey to loving your body and yourself, skillfully weaving personal anecdotes into the story. Her words have a transformative impact, promoting a healthy self-image. Mothers will find this book to be a valuable resource in breaking the cycle of poor body image, lack of self-esteem, and low self-confidence, creating a positive legacy for their daughters. A true gem for anyone seeking a path to loving themselves and their bodies."

– **Maria Fuller**, Founder of Raising a Powerful Girl

"I love this book! As a Dr. of Holistic Health with over 23 years experience I have listened to countless women say I will be happy when...Marla's story is a perfect example of the fallacy of this belief. When... rarely comes and if it does I have yet to see its promise delivered. In *Be Friend Yourself*, Marla shows you the path back to loving and accepting yourself in the now. The secret, I have found, to creating lasting health and vibrancy in your body. It is a must read for anyone struggling to accept their body!"

– **Dr. Cari Schaefer**

BE-FRIEND
YOURSELF

BE-FRIEND
YOURSELF

Finding Freedom with Food
and Peace with your Body

Marla Mervis-Hartmann

BE-Friend Yourself: Finding Freedom with Food and Peace with your Body

© 2024 by Marla Mervis-Hartmann

All rights reserved. No portion of this publication may be reproduced, stored in a retrieval system, or transmitted by any means—electronic, mechanical, photocopying, recording, or any other—except for brief quotations in printed reviews, without the prior written permission of the publisher.

The events depicted in this book are based upon the author's memories of them and any unwitting errors that may appear are the author's own. Some names and details have been changed to protect privacy.

Editors: Mary Ward Menke, Noëlla Simmons
Cover and Interior Design: Emma Elzinga
Cover Photo by Vizerskaya from iStock.com

3 West Garden Street, Ste. 718
Pensacola, FL 32502
www.indigoriverpublishing.com

Ordering Information:

Quantity sales: Special discounts are available on quantity purchases by corporations, associations, and others. For details, contact the publisher at the address above.

Orders by US trade bookstores and wholesalers: Please contact the publisher at the address above.

Printed in the United States of America

Library of Congress Control Number: 2024907695
ISBN: 978-1954676916 (paperback)   978-1954676923 (ebook)

First Edition

With Indigo River Publishing, you can always expect great books, strong voices, and meaningful messages. Most importantly, you'll always find . . . *words worth reading.*

Contents

To my nieces.
Love,
Aunt Marla

Foreword

What is it to be a friend to one's own body? Why would we want to be friends with something that we so often can't stand? In a culture bound by body shame, orthorexia, junk food, and cosmetic surgery, the concept of loving our bodies can feel nearly impossible. Religion, culture, and capitalism have rendered the human connection to the body as something severed, cut off at the neck. What happens below is a mystery, is not to be felt. The body is seen as a vessel, the site of sin, monstrous—something we must woefully drag around with us on our earthly journey until we can transcend. Oh, but to see what a beautiful gift to be alive in the body we are given! What a miracle it is to feel at home within oneself.

Marla Mervis-Hartmann is no stranger to the conflict that lives within our very cells—the desire to look and feel perfect butted up against the soft beauty of our perfectly imperfect forms. Marla's own journey taught her to be in relationship with her body, to learn to treat herself with the compassion and empathy of a very good friend. No longer was her body something she had to "work on" to "perfect"; rather, through a process of self-love, healing, and deep emotional transformation, she was able to radically shift her beliefs about her body, her food, her fitness, and most importantly, her worth.

Now, Marla offers her wisdom to others seeking to transform their body-self relationship, and she does so with the heart of a best friend who is always looking out for the ones she loves most. Her work as a coach powerfully blends her own experiences, her extensive professional training, a reiki practice, and cutting-edge somatic strategies to serve her clientele in life-changing ways.

I am fortunate to be one of Marla's clients, and over the past several years of working together, Marla has helped me shift from a mindset of shame, mistrust, and self-punishment, to realizing that my God-given body is my most precious relationship. After my initiation into motherhood, my body-self relationship shifted greatly—a difficult pregnancy, birth, and postpartum will do that. Even years later, that relationship had not recovered. I did not feel at home in myself. My body felt like someone who had betrayed me, and I didn't know if I could ever forgive. I was at a breaking point in my relationship to myself, my marriage, and my career. I knew I needed to do something different, so I reached out to Marla.

Marla and I had met many years prior at a women's sexual wellness training where we were both participants. Her beautiful energy was clear to me those years ago, and I was in awe of how deeply she opened up to our group about her own journey as a woman and a mother. I was not yet a mother at the time, but as a doula, I found the experience powerful. Years later, when I spoke to one of our cohort classmates about the state of my life and body postpartum, she said I must work with Marla, and that she had been seeing her for coaching. Though it had been a long time since we were in the training together, the image of her sharing her birth with us still remained in my mind. I felt like she was the one I needed at this time, to hold me as I came back to myself.

And has she! Marla leads with the body in all aspects of life. What one may think is coaching for body image or food goes so much deeper. I knew my life was not in balance and that my body was feeling the brunt of it. Years of night nursing and co-sleeping had my hormones and thyroid zapped—I was falling asleep randomly and my knees were killing me. I was irritable and not giving the world the best of me. Marla helped me remember how to listen. How to get quiet with my body and hear its messages, pleas, and requests. She helped me remember how to love and care for myself above all else. Motherhood, especially in this culture, asks us to put ourselves on the back burner, and I needed someone to hold me (sometimes drag me!) to the forefront of my own priorities. What I love about Marla is that, while she is tender and gentle, she is not afraid to reflect back what *is*, and she is not afraid to push when a stubborn client (such as myself) needs it. I have learned so much through our work together, many tools for coping with anger, dysregulation, self-image, and work stress, but most importantly I have learned who I am, and who I want to be.

Marla has encouraged me to create a relationship with food that is nourishing for the body I now live in—helping me grieve the loss of gluten (it's not easy!), and affirming all of the positive changes I have made to take the best care I can of myself. And when, amidst all of my hard work and progress, I was hit by a car while crossing the street one Sunday morning, I had Marla with me for the months I spent living in bed with a broken foot and ankle. She was instrumental in helping me process and reduce the trauma of that experience, not to mention survive the mental toll of having to pause my career, cease my exercise program, and significantly adjust my ability to care for my family. I could not have gotten through that experience without her loving care, wisdom, and insight. (And reiki!)

This work is deep and it permeates into every corner of a woman's life—it isn't something one should do alone or without another wise woman to walk the path with you. Marla's book serves as a beautiful guide to traverse the course to healing and self-love, but if you can, I hope you will choose to work with Marla in all the other beautiful ways she offers the world. Her ability to support women in trusting and loving themselves is profound, and I attribute our work together to the improvements I have seen with my relationship to food and wellness, as well as in other areas of my life. It has given me tools for teaching my young daughter to love her body, and undoubtedly has helped me with my own clients as well. I hope this book serves you well, reader, and that through this important work you are doing, you come to love your body and yourself as well, always!

Zoë Etkin
Somatic Coach & Bodyworker
Author of *The Mother Myths*

Introduction

On a scale of one to ten, one being *Absolutely not*, and ten being *Hell yes*, tell me, how much do you love your body? Vulnerably speaking, I have lived most of my life in the lower digits: the twos and threes. Although my God-given body was strong, fit, and healthy, I spent decades lamenting that it was not *perfect*. Those years of grief catapulted me into a toxic relationship with my appearance that resulted in decades of compulsive eating, restricting, bingeing, purging, and dieting.

Some people are surprised to hear this. "Really, you?" they'll ask. "But you always seem so confident; I had no idea you were struggling with body and food challenges too!"

Yes. Me.

My journey through self-acceptance has been the most plaguing and rewarding lesson of my life. Because I have existed within the same fifteen-pound range, it's been easy to hide my struggles with the scale and obsession about my body.

Like most women, my grievances with my weight were seeded at a young age. I grew up as one of those curvy little girls that people would make comments about—words that later influenced me to believe I needed to look a certain way.

In my teenage years, I played sports, which put a great deal of demand on my body. Then, I was an actor and a dancer, so once again . . . different expectations, but *more* physical demands. Although, I, for the most part, had body confidence in my high school years, these consistent messages and experiences regarding my appearance left me confused and vulnerable to a disordered relationship with food and my body.

So, by college, the cocktail of unrealistic body standards and societal pressure around dieting thrust me into a sea of toxic beliefs, negative self-talk, and destructive behaviors around my weight. Diet culture is so invasive and rooted into the fabric of our existence that it is rarely visible until you step back to take a thoughtful look at it.

So, what *is* diet culture?

Christy Harrison, MPH, RD, author of *The Anti-Diet*, defines "diet culture" as: "a belief system that worships thinness and equates it to health and moral virtue, promotes weight loss and maintaining a low weight as a way to elevate social status, and demonizes certain foods and eating styles while elevating others."

According to Harrison, diet culture also "oppresses people who don't match up with its supposed picture of 'health,' which disproportionately harms women, femmes, trans folks, people in larger bodies, people of color, and people with disabilities."[1]

My tools to deal with these pressures, in addition to the traumas and emotions of life were adversely handled by dieting and eating. I will go into these stories with open honesty in this book. I created this book to share my experience so that you don't have to suffer so long and hard.

The trouble with diet culture is that only about 5 percent of women can actually live up to that standard of beauty, and the rest of us are left to feel bad about ourselves. Furthermore, I didn't realize how deeply anchored the fear of being "fat" is woven into the fabric of our culture. Its roots primarily stem from racism and religious pressures for pious eating.

Harrison covers this as well in her book: "As important as evolutionary theory was when it came to explaining how we all came to be on this planet, it was also used in overtly racist ways, to justify the white Anglo-European male domination of other cultures and genders

---

1   Harrison, Christy. *The Anti-Diet*. Little, Brown Spark, 2019.

that had been going on for centuries. Evolutionary theory became a 'scientific' way of upholding the status quo. White, Northern European women were deemed to be a step down from men on the evolutionary ladder, followed by Southern Europeans (again with the women a step down from the men), then people of color from countries that early biologists and anthropologists considered 'semicivilized' or 'barbaric,' and finally, at the bottom, Native Americans and Africans, whom they considered 'savages.'"[2]

Therein, the positive body image, anti-diet, and fat liberation movements are fighting back against deep systemic racism and privilege. Finally, women are standing up and saying *No more*. No more ancestral trauma. No more generational oppression. We will evolve past our grandmothers and mothers through the *radical* embrace of our bodies. We will be unapologetic about eating delicious food that nourishes our body—*knowing* we are doing something revolutionary.

It is my intention with this book to help people feel better in their own skin, to make peace with food, and to have a thriving life. As a thin, white, privileged, cisgender woman, I will do my best to make this message serve you, the reader. I don't pretend to understand the sufferings of transgender, binary, and other marginalized cultures. But I do hope you feel my highest desire to support those loving themselves deeper. Throughout this book, I address my readers as "women." I mean any sister who identifies as a woman: cis women, trans women, women who have yet to reveal their internal gender to the external world. I also invite non-binary and male readers into the fold. After all, fatphobia, diet culture, and systemic body shaming impacts everyone in deeply personal ways. I pray that you feel welcome here and supported by my journey.

From an early age, I didn't know why it was so hard to like my body. I wasn't aware that loving and caring for myself was an act of power that challenges a damaging societal view to girls and women. When we take back our power around our weight and bodies—when

---

2   Harrison, Christy. *The Anti-Diet*. Little, Brown Spark, 2019.

we heal—we become activists in the fight against diet culture and its toxic origins. Every time we acknowledge our worth has nothing to do with our appearance, we revolt against deep systemic beliefs that tell us being a certain size matters.

The benefit of our culture growing into new knowledge is being able to articulate these issues with new terms. My disordered eating likely would have gone undefined prior to the 1990s. I took my inability to be *perfect* to the extreme to something we now call *exercise bulimia*. While *bulimia* is a bingeing and purging cycle, *exercise bulimia* is working out until complete exhaustion if you eat . . . *anything*. My logic was: *what goes in must be burnt off*. I was obsessed with food, diet, and exhausting myself.

From the outside, it appeared as though I loved to be fit; that I loved going to the gym and eating healthy. In reality, my mental health was in the toilet. All of my motivation came from feelings of disgust about myself, the belief that my body *was not good enough*. I believed the lie diet culture was teaching me: *I cannot be happy unless . . .*

Unless I'm the perfect weight.

Unless I'm the ideal size.

Unless I burn a certain number of calories.

I had support. I had a privileged life with an amazing family. I was loved, popular, and mostly liked myself, but at times—peace wasn't present. I might have one good week, become stressed by something, then spiral into being unkind to myself. There were certainly days I felt stunning, sexy, and in shape—but if I had a second cookie, my feelings would instantly shift. Having an erratic relationship with my appearance set the stage for keeping a tight grip on my food intake and giving airtime to an inner critic who loved to tell me all the ways I fell short.

Back then, there wasn't a popularized term for this pattern of behavior. Today, I would most likely have been identified as an *orthorexic*: a person who is preoccupied with healthy rituals to an unhealthy measure. Researchers now see this with women who become overly concerned with nutrients, ingredients, and chemicals—taking their tunnel vision about calories, carbs, and fats too far. The condition is a complete addiction to finding the healthiest way to do everything—from eating, to grooming, to self-care. In reality, it creates a lot of mental noise that serves no one.[3]

This thinking robbed me of years of satisfaction and joy. I missed out on so much, including learning how to celebrate my womanhood and femininity. It resulted in an inability to really *enjoy* my relationship with food, sex, and myself.

Through years of misery that landed me at my own dark night of the soul, I decided it was time for a change, and took a vested interest in the way I spoke to myself. This is when I adopted the concept of Be-*Friending myself*—which ultimately broke the seal of wild possibility in every area of my life.

Once I could show up and give myself what I deserved, there was no room any longer to settle for anything below my worth. I'd ask myself, "Marla—would you speak to a friend the way you're speaking to yourself right now?"

If the answer was *no*, I'd use my tools (that you will learn in this book) to make myself feel better.

It wasn't easy, and it took a while to get used to my own inner dialogue changes, but over time I learned to enjoy being nice to myself.

Soon, I began exploring new ways to celebrate my life. I started practicing movement, energy work, creative self-expression, and healing from the inside out. Eventually, I was able to divorce myself from societal concepts that were not serving me—things like toxic diet culture, shame around my sexuality, the no pain, no gain: American mentality, and the notion that I didn't deserve nourishment or rest *unless* I checked all the boxes.

Where I was once overly concerned and regimented, I now respect my attempt to show up for myself as a practice. I'm evolving. It doesn't always come naturally. I still have to work at it, but this process has been integral to my establishing a sense of peace.

---

3   Scarff J. R. (2017). Orthorexia Nervosa: An Obsession With Healthy Eating. *Federal practitioner: for the health care professionals of the VA, DoD, and PHS, 34* (6), 36–39.

By stepping into my enoughness, and deciding against all odds I am going to partner with myself, I became my own best friend.

Throughout that time, this is what I realized:

- A good friend listens. So, I learned to listen to my body, be more attentive to its cues, defend its boundaries, and grant its request for nourishment, food, water, movement, and pleasure.

- A good friend is there for you.

- A good friend doesn't even have to say anything. In fact, she senses your need for silence, and she's good with that. She wants to be there for you. Because she loves you.

- A good friend prioritizes your comfort.

- A good friend is respectful of boundaries around your time, space, and energy.

- A good friend forgives. Can we forgive ourselves?

- A good friend accepts our greatness and our flaws.

- A good friend speaks the truth in love, kindness, and compassion.

I knew, more than anything, I wanted to love myself like that. I wanted to embrace all the things that made me Marla, and all the things I'd not yet explored about my femininity. I wanted to speak kindly to myself, to accept my greatness and my flaws, to unapologetically prioritize my needs, and above all—to heal through radical self-forgiveness while giving my own heart and mind the benefit of the doubt. Through this new sense of liberation and profound self-compassion, I also realized—*I wanted to teach what I was coming to understand.* I wanted to help other women learn to embrace the nourishment of food and the joy of celebrating their bodies.

I remember sitting on the floor in my friend's bedroom in Kauai. I was nine months pregnant with my son, sharing the beauty and labors of womanhood with someone safe, who wholeheartedly understood.

There, I was struck with: *This is your purpose, Marla. Take all of your fears, wisdom, struggles, and triumphs and share them with others.*

Finally. My pain had a silver lining. Finally. I felt like I could let go of restriction, and encourage others to do the same.

I'd already been *very* committed to sharing what I knew about women's health. But at that moment, I knew my purpose was to combine my knowledge as a Reiki master, tantra teacher, yogi, and somatic trauma specialist to help people heal their relationship with food and their bodies.

Now my life's work is encouraging women to quiet the militant inner critic that lives inside their heads. My body still gets covered in goosebumps when my clients and friends choose freedom over restriction. As I sat there, beaming with my happy, pregnant belly I heard the words, *love your body, love yourself.* I knew then that would be my business and my mission. I was pregnant with Aspen, and the seed of a second growing, vibrant, perseverant dream.

I don't know about you, but I think women are pretty phenomenal. And when I say "women," I mean this for *every person* who considers themselves a member of the sisterhood. We *all* bear our unique scars when it comes to femininity; which is why I'm dedicated to working with women of every shape, size, color, and background. There's one thing in particular about women that I believe makes them amazing: they are *healers.*

Women are empathetic.

Dynamic.

Kind.

Feminine.

Daring.

Beautiful.

And beyond that—they love and partner with intention. If something's broken, they want to talk about it, learn from it, and heal it. A woman's resiliency is usually her strongest attribute. It didn't take long in this work to realize I had everything I needed to heal myself already wrapped up in my own femininity.

It all began with going inward: tuning in, turning on, and listening . . . first to the cues of my body, then to my intuition, childhood wounds, quieted dreams, bold inspirations, and the sound of my own vibrant heart. *There are so many layers* of ourselves to celebrate if we will just take the time to *listen*.

The more we hear our inner truths, the more we create synergy within our body. As we step into flow, we position ourselves to expand—to experience pleasure, to have fun, and to thrive in our fullest potential.

And so, I invite you to be honest with yourself. On a scale of one to ten, how much do you love yourself?

Maybe right now, you are at a one or a two when it comes to loving your body. You know what? That's okay! Take a moment to live in your authentic experience. But by the end of our work together, my hope is that you will be able to enjoy the glorious sensation of basking in your own magnificence. It may seem counterintuitive at first—after years of being hard on myself, it took time to establish a sense of safety and trust. But that's why I'm here: to remind you of your own brilliance when you aren't quite sure of it yet, and to support you on your journey to becoming your own best friend.

1

Be Authentic

"A friend is one who overlooks your broken fence, and
admires the flowers in your garden."
– *Unknown*

My young life was a great life. I was raised in a healthy, loving home with warm parents who celebrated my sisters and me. As we grew up, we were told we were beautiful. We were dressed in stylish school clothes each fall, loved to pamper ourselves, and were solid in our sense of self-esteem. I never had an issue making friends. In my teenage years, I got dates easily; boys regularly showed interest in me. I was popular, *and* a good student, *and* I soared in activities that thrust me into the spotlight. In theater, I loved center stage. I put myself out there, took risks, and excelled at public speaking.

This is why, after most of my close friends hear my story, they give feedback along the lines of: *Wow! I didn't know you had that trauma.*

I can't believe you struggled with body confidence.

I'm so sorry. I didn't know you were suffering.

I always find it difficult to respond, because—while everyone experiences trauma—I can honestly say nothing distressing plagued my childhood. I *was* born confident and was encouraged in that self-assurance by my parents, who thought the world of me. I wasn't in the throes of suffering *all the time*; however, I'd learned to use food and my body to cope with life's struggles.

For those on the outside, this insight can be confusing because they assume I wouldn't feel this way for a multitude of reasons. Still, negative body image doesn't discriminate with body size. You can be any shape, size, age, or gender and feel negatively about yourself. My intention is to bring awareness to the process that has less to do with our body and food, and more to do with our mind and heart. These steps incite the deep healing work that signals permission to live an authentic, thriving, pleasureful life.

Throughout my career in the healing arts, I have done more workshops than I can count. If there's one thing I know about stories in our culture, it's that people *crave* a rags-to-riches narrative. I could easily sell my audience on something that was partially true, but in doing so I'd miss the opportunity to relate to *every woman* who has *ever wondered* if her pain is valid enough.

To present my advantaged upbringing as a story of distress would be a lie, but to say that it hasn't been tremendously difficult to heal my relationship with food would also be a lie. So, I choose to be honest. I choose to honor myself— share stories from my past that perhaps aren't the most harrowing narratives in the world but were certainly *hard enough* to affect my relationship with my body.

In my practice, I work with people who fall into four basic categories:

- Those who are on a healing journey with their body and food.

- Those who are ensnared in disordered eating patterns, who see they have a problem, but do not know how to help themselves.

- Those who are ensnared in disordered eating patterns, who do not see that they have a problem, and have no intention to help themselves.

- Those who want to heal their body image and recognize it starts from the inside out.

If you're reading this book and identify with one of these categories but feel isolated on your journey—this work is for you! My content is designed to get to the heart of *all* troubled relationships with food and body image by addressing *all* the influences that keep people stuck in unhealthy patterns. This content is for everyone! We do not have to succumb to a *just okay* relationship with ourselves or our bodies. In fact, the bulk of my writing and seminars are rooted in the principles of Be-*Friending ourselves.*

Think of it this way: if you were sitting across the table from your best friend, telling her your story, being vulnerable about your relationship with food, what would she say? I can only hope she wouldn't invalidate your experience by emphasizing *just how well you have it.* Because ladies, that's not friendship.

A good friend listens.

A good friend empathizes.

A good friend is supportive.

Are you a good friend to yourself?

By the completion of this book, I want my readers to be able to assess their relationships with their appearance and believe that the painful experiences that set these patterns into motion *are valid* no matter how small they seem. It is my hope that by reading my story, I can give you full permission to feel yourself and move through your past and present experiences so you can love yourself more. To learn to listen to that small authentic voice inside that is aching to be heard. My friend, my prayer is for your full liberation from the pain of negative food behaviors and body image.

Something to consider throughout this book is that our upbringing largely defines how we will feel about our bodies into adulthood—*even* if we are privileged and grow up in an excellent home. This was the case with my childhood; for which I am grateful—but also acknowledge those unhealthy messages *still* had impact, even if I was loved. I grew up in a small town outside of Pittsburgh, Pennsylvania, a sister to two vibrant girls who were as beautiful and smart as I was. My parents adored us. We had tons of friends and were good at most things. By every definition we had a charmed childhood, complete with grass-stained knees, freedom to run around the neighborhood until dark, playing dress-up with friends, eating popsicles on the porch, dancing with sprinklers in the summer, and playing and sleeping in beautifully decorated bedrooms.

Still, I struggled with the social pressure to *be* a certain way. I don't know many females who escape the crippling fear that their bodies are wrong at any age. Early on, we are inundated with the lie that our bodies are the key to our happiness. It makes us competitive—with ourselves and with other girls.

By junior high, I was sharp and accomplished—always the top of my class, a leader in student council, an elected member of the homecoming court, and a star on the school theater stage. *Authentically*, this was me. *This was Marla.*

I've always been vibrant and expressive, and I'll admit it—I've always enjoyed the attention with a microphone in hand. Sadly, this backfired on more than one occasion during my teenage years. Unfortunately, my love for the spotlight often evoked feelings of inadequacy and jealousy in my female friends. Usually, these feelings would manifest in hurtful interactions that left me feeling confused about how to act and *be* in the world.

It began with eighth grade superlative nominations where the class was instructed to vote for *most likely to succeed, prettiest hair*, and *best athlete*. As I sat at my desk poring over the results, I found my name elected in several categories. My eyes twinkled! I quietly sat at my desk, excited to go home and show my mom. It had been such a good day; I felt confident, supported, and beautiful!

Then suddenly, one of my good friends approached my desk. Her color changed quickly as she looked over my shoulder reading the results. She went from cheerful to sneering in a matter of seconds and said, "You don't deserve to be in so many categories. Beauty is in the eye of the beholder!"

At first, I was confused. Then I was shocked. Then angry. Then sad.

Very sad. I wanted to cry for my friend; I was heartbroken that she hadn't gotten many votes, that I was in the spotlight. I loved her, and she was being hard on herself simply because I existed. I felt embarrassed that I had been voted so many times, and though it wasn't my fault, I felt ashamed. By the end of the conversation, I felt so small I wanted to crawl under my desk.

When the bell rang, I crumpled up the piece of paper and shoved it into my backpack.

The following limiting beliefs took root that day, and they stayed with me into my adult years:

If I am myself, I will hurt other people.

If I take up space, it will influence others to shrink.

If I feel pretty, it will cause others pain.

If I celebrate myself, it will offend the people I love.

I had what most women have but do not know how to articulate or manage—an array of overwhelming messages that I could not sort out:

You are special, but do not revel in it.

You are loved, but do not get too comfortable.

You are a star, but make sure not to eclipse others.

You are allowed to be yourself, until you make others uncomfortable.

This is how it begins, and usually at an age where we're too young to have conversations with our mothers about it. As a sweet, pleasing middle child, I wanted *everyone* to like me. When they didn't, I punished myself by turning that rejection inward; I relied on food and body obsession as a way to self-soothe—searching for something to bring me a sense of clarity and control.

I know, I know. You might be thinking, *Poor you! You got attention because you were pretty, people liked you, and you were good at things!*

The reality is—the positive attention didn't negate the painful attention. Until now, I held back on telling my story because to the people who love me, it will be tragic, and to the people who do not know me, it will not be tragic enough. So, I share this to serve my authentic self, and I encourage my readers to follow in my footsteps.

As we let go of our negative thoughts surrounding food and press into healing our relationship with our bodies, I challenge you to consider your *why*. If your initial thought still is, *I want to lose weight*, it's time to get real with yourself—I urge you to go deeper. Try to make your *why* more prominent than your weight. It's a hollow journey.

The only time I was able to successfully surrender foods for good was doing it as a genuine act of compassion. My higher self was calling the shots, not my inner critic—my sanity was prioritized over my waistline; only then did my waistline follow suit. And I *still* delight in what I love.

Right now, as I sip a delicious, chocolate cookie milkshake, I ask you, *what is your why?* Even better if you have a couple! But make them specific, and cling to them.

And consider the following questions:

Why do you want to have a happy relationship with food?

Why do you want to eat healthier foods or allow yourself my indulgences?

Why do you want to stop emotional eating and look at it differently?

What is your *why* behind the bigger *why*?

Now, write it down. Read it out loud. Make sure it resonates and isn't someone else's bright idea. Let's get real here, people, can we? I challenge you to be courageous with your vision, and allow yourself to get messy in the process—be bold, be *bad*, and most importantly, be true to the you that deserves to taste life to the fullest with every bite!

Sure, I was already a coach, Reiki master, speaker and body worker, but I didn't know an innate part of my purpose would be writing and serving you! I have known that self-love was always the answer, but it was not until I moved into deeper healing that I understood my story could influence the way women see themselves. In turn, sharing about my relationship with my body—for better and for worse—is the one thing I have set out to do. I hope it can be as life-changing for you as it has been for me.

2

Be Enough

"One of the greatest regrets in life is being what others
would want you to be, rather than being yourself."
– *Shannon L. Alder*

We were having dinner at my mom's house with both sides of the family. Both my uncle and cousin are runners who love working out. My stomach sank, and my chest grew tight as they shared about their workouts: Although it was a mere ten to fifteen minutes, it felt like eternity. "I like to start out with my run and end with light stretching and twenty minutes of abs." As my cousin said this, a sense of familiar dread crept up in my throat.

Constantly comparing myself to others, I became acutely aware of the feeling of my pants pressing against my stomach and the way my body was heavier than my cousin's. They made exercise sound enjoyable. My dysfunctional relationship with working out was anything but fun. Exercise meant pushing myself to exhaustion to burn off extra calories.

Shut up, already! I wanted to scream, but instead I kept a smile pasted on my face. As I pressed my chair back from the table, my mom set a hearty bowl of mashed potatoes in front of us—a basin deep enough to cradle my nosedive of shame. I resorted to rapidly shoveling heaps of carbs in my mouth as they continued their conversation, while both of them were denying helpings of the side dish. The more I ate, the more horrible I felt. The more horrible I felt, the more I ate.

My triggers were everywhere. An innocent family conversation about sit-ups could launch into a state of fight-or-flight. The attractive woman dancing with unbridled pleasure at my dance class made me seethe out of nowhere. An Instagram post displaying a "before" and "after" photo of an old college friend, compelled me to look up a cleanse for the following weekend. If you relate to this experience, I bet your triggers feel like they are out to get you too. I empathize because they can make us feel quite unsafe.

It's easy to fall into the comparison trap. We observe beautiful women, and we think their polished appearance renders something about us—*not enough*. We think because we have a different style, alternative approach, or a more relaxed pace that we are somehow *deficient* or *other*. My habit of old was walking down the street, continually catching glimpses of myself in store windows and comparing myself to women around me.

What do I look like?

Am I as thin as the girl in front of me?

My criticism of myself and my criticism of others got so out of control at times, I couldn't reel it in. Moreover, I didn't want to reel it in; tempering it might mean losing control. And despite feeling depleted and vain, I was addicted—to shame. When my self-critical thoughts were really bad, I would find myself lashing out at people around me. Living in Los Angeles, yelling at the surrounding cars on the interstate was my favorite way to unleash my rage. Granted, road rage never ends well. Especially when you eventually realize the person in the other car is your friend from yoga class . . . *guilty*!

In my calmer moments, I'd coerce myself into accepting myself the way I was. It was completely guilt-induced, and showed no real compassion toward my body at all.

Stop it, Marla, your body is merely the shell for a soul! I'd say, sassing myself out of my own inner dialogue, knowing somehow it was only perpetuating the cycle.

While I knew my soul made me beautiful, I couldn't stop looking in the mirror and scowling. I was ashamed of myself for my thoughts, my behavior, and well—pretty much any and everything I could make into being my fault. Even if something was someone else's fault, I could flip it internally and give myself something to eat about. That's shame for you—a vicious cycle that deteriorates compassion. I was always on a mission for self-condemnation, I was my own worst enemy.

I can't believe I ate my whole sandwich at lunch. That girl across from me only ate half of hers. I need to exercise tonight, and I don't care how tired I am. I can feel the extra flesh on my stomach. So gross!

Of course, I couldn't share any of this with anyone. I was certain they would call me crazy *because I was acting crazy!* So, I kept my thoughts and behaviors to myself.

When I think about all the time that I spent obsessing about my body, the food I was—or was not—going to consume, and planning my exercise—I grieve the time I lost. Sometimes this manifests as anger or sadness. It's all part of the healing process. I acknowledge that I robbed myself of some of my more precious moments.

Instead of enjoying a sexy date with my boyfriend, I would pick a fight because I was hungry and emotional and didn't want to feel bad about the way I looked.

"You look beautiful," he'd say.

"Whatever. You're just saying that because you have to . . ." I'd respond in irritation; angry that he even brought up the way I looked, because I didn't want to accept myself. I'd tell him to leave, and then when he'd go—I'd punish myself by bingeing. The cycle was unending, and touched everything significant to me. Over time, it started keeping me from my professional pursuits.

I would starve myself before a musical audition. If my outfit didn't fit my silhouette perfectly, I would cancel interviews. I'd deny myself the opportunity to journal about my dreams and desires for the future, and would instead make a list of recipes and diets to follow. *Why go out and live when you can make a board about bone broth fasting on Pinterest?*

I was always rehearsing life and preparing my body for a role I was never beautiful enough—by my own standards—to play. Years passed, and the curtain never went up. I was always *becoming* and never *being* in my enough-ness—never existing in the moment.

I didn't know it, but I desperately needed a wake-up call. I've worked with women long enough to be able to champion myself internally to some degree. So, I'd attempt to rev myself up, *Sister, check yourself. Stop it. Snap out of your crazy thoughts!* I'd say to myself.

But these bursts of manic encouragement never seemed to bring long-lasting relief. They were only surface affirmations unable to tap my internal well of brooding anger. The highs and lows of this pattern would instigate bingeing and overexercising. Deprivation could make me feel accomplished in a way nothing else did. One meal a day was a *thin day*. If I caved to temptation and ate a snack before bed, the whole plan was a wash—and I was nothing again.

What can we do when we find ourselves in this dreadful cycle? Well, first, we can recognize that shame begets shame; we must stop beating ourselves the moment we realize we are doing it. If we can turn our self-talk upside down with self-compassion—which ultimately brings us into the present.

According to shame expert, Dr. Brené Brown, "If you put Shame in a Petri dish, it needs three things to grow exponentially: secrecy, silence, and judgment. If you put the same amount of shame in a Petri dish and douse it with empathy, it can't survive." [4]

Addressing shame is key to finding freedom and forgiveness—with ourselves, and sometimes with the past. Shame never inspires affirmative action. In the spirit of shame, we shrink, hide, then take negative steps to make something *right* that can only be made *healthy*—by *love*.

The years of constant obsessing about food and my body left me feeling empty and sore. I could never access a complete source of comfort outside myself; I didn't understand the acceptance I was looking for

---

4   Brown, Brené. *Dare to Lead Brave Work. Tough Conversations.* Whole Hearts Ebury Digital, 2019.

could only come from within. After getting sick and tired of being sick and tired, I acknowledged I had to find a way to stop the insanity. To get to the root of the obsession, I had to get to the root of the shame. To get to the root of the shame, I intuited I had to stop the secrecy. So, I courageously began speaking out my feelings to loosen the judgment.

I feel angry. I don't feel justified about being angry. That makes me feel angrier.

I feel sad. I don't understand why, which makes me feel confused and impatient.

I feel tired all the time, and that exhaustion makes me feel resentful.

I feel shame at the fact that I feel so many feelings.

As I held space for myself, I allowed the emotions to flow through me, like a river, without judgment.

My practice influenced me to consider this additional sentiment from Dr. Brown:

"Shame says, 'I am bad.' Guilt says, 'I did something bad.'" [5]

I adopted this notion and applied it to my relationship with food. The cycle was just my behavior. It was not a reflection of my character. In other words, I am still an amazing, powerful, loving woman even if I stuffed myself on pizza.

This helped me consider bingeing from a more objective perspective. Removing the emotion helped me see that compulsive eating made me feel tired, achy, and swollen. Even with a food hangover, I'd cancel all plans so I would exercise off the shame of eating. These symptoms would fuel the negative thoughts that would make me question my worth further. When I could separate my behavior from my value, my healing began.

During this process, I started speaking to myself kindly. I'd correct my course with something like, *Oh Marla. I am sorry that you feel binge-eating is the answer. What's happening to make you binge-eat? I am sad that you are comparing yourself to others and can't see your beauty. I want you to accept*

---

5   Brown, Brené. *Daring Greatly: How the Courage to Be Vulnerable Transforms the Way We Live, Love, Parent, and Lead.* Penguin Random House Audio Publishing Group, 2017.

yourself. I want you to know how your worth is bigger than your body. You may not see that right now. What would help you feel better?

My responses would often surprise me. Sometimes I needed to be held or craved a walk or wanted to drink some hot tea. I learned to self-soothe, instead of self-punish—usually tempering my emotions with things other than food.

Most of my clients want me to be a disciplinarian. They approach me, eager to adopt a list of activities that will mitigate their binge-eating. When I give them exercises to address their shame, they are sorely disappointed.

Don't I need to throw out all my snack foods? Can't I just go for a walk? they'll ask.

No. The key is getting to the core of our shame and uprooting it.

It all begins with changing our self-talk, I'll say.

Talk about a buzzkill—*we must be nice to ourselves?* Yes, it's a bummer, I know.

The best way to stop the binge-eating is to kill the shame around it. We need to stop making the behavior *mean* something about ourselves. If you indulge in a beer and burger—guess what? That's okay, in fact, I'd even identify that as yummy!

Furthermore, you're not a felon. You don't have to pay penance, nor be your own emotional jailor. You didn't harm anyone, or threaten anyone's life, you didn't light a building on fire, or commit a hit and run. You don't have to self-flagellate. In fact, the faster you move on, the faster you can stop the cycle.

Additionally, your bounce back rate and pace is important to your healing process. I say that with compassion in an attempt to meet every person who struggles with disordered eating where they are. It's painful, no doubt. But you are all the more powerful. And a voice inside you is waiting to be heard—a truth, is begging to be told. So, I care more about your authenticity than anything else. If I could reveal my truths, you can too. In fact, I can't wait to hear what you have to say.

I also encourage my clients to stop being obsessed with their own obsession.

I'm crazy, why can't I stop these thoughts? is pretty self-deprecating. Instead, I recommend taking self-inventory. Be gentle when asking yourself questions—the way you would a close friend, or a small child.

Why is this weighing so heavily on you? What do you feel is the most challenging part? Is there anything I can do to help?

It's our responsibility to nurture ourselves and tend to our needs with curiosity and care instead of impatience and judgment.

Everyone has needs, and they are nothing to be ashamed of. Needs do not equal "neediness," nor is your amount of need an indicator of your worth. If you require someone else's permission to meet your own needs, consider this your prescription:

Take one dose of acceptance for your feelings in the morning, a capsule of self-compassion and self-talk in the afternoon, and a long drink of gratitude before bed.

Offer an action statement as a prescription rather than an analysis. For example, the prescription here might be: Give yourself whatever you most need at this moment.

The minute I find myself second-guessing my worth by making a snide remark to myself while putting my jeans on, I do a check-in. It's usually a sign a negative weed has grown out of control, and needs to be pulled out at the root. I do my best to tend to my own mental and emotional garden, then I keep moving forward. Over time, my headspace becomes a more pleasant place to be. I become acutely aware of what's harming me, and I no longer allow those beliefs to grow.

Sometimes, we all get scared—and guess what? That's okay. In fact, I've learned that the demons in the dark were actually parts of myself that were scared. When I searched in my closet for the skeletons, I found younger pieces of myself that needed attention. Part of healing from obsession is inviting these younger *Marlas* out of my closet, and to the dinner table. I give them a name.

Hello, Fear of Failure. Have a seat. Would you like to talk about your feelings?

What about you, little one who has Fear of Abandonment? You have space to express yourself here.

The constant dinner guest in my life was Fear of Being Unlovable. In turn, I was always making sure that I was accepted by those around me. I *needed* to be liked and turned myself inside out to not upset anyone. I believed that if I upset someone then I was unlovable.

Each week, I saved it a seat at the head of the table—just to prove to myself I was worthy of deep adoration, regardless of my successes, failures, and appearance. The more I faced my inner child, the more I could BE-Friend myself. I stopped feeling eclipsed by negative beliefs. I could walk into yoga proud—without even a thought about how my body looked, fully content with myself, when in the past, I was constantly checking myself out in the mirror and comparing myself to others.

Warrior pose began to feel natural. The urge to shrink dissipated as I allowed myself to take up space—to consider my deeper cause. Then, I could show up for myself, as an advocate and a healer, allowing forgiveness to soften my heart and smooth my edges.

Through inner child work, I learned we get stuck at different ages. In times of stress, we regress to our childhood pains. So, if you find yourself lashing out like a toddler during a spat, you might actually be reverting back to the pain of your youngest years. Little you accessing the coping skills of your inner two-year-old. She may be upset and need to be held. Just like we can talk to our emotional states, we can talk to our inner children at different stages. I might say, "Little Marla, are you okay? Do you need to be held? I am here for you."

Though children have big feelings, for the most part, tending to their aches is much easier than the mental processing we do as adults. For example, Aspen recently got angry at a friend for playfully throwing a rock at him. *Rightfully so!* But still, the kid didn't *mean* anything by it. As Aspen relayed his frustration, I held space for all his big and lingering feelings, and he was able to fully release his upset. Had I diminished his feeling and made him rush into *forgiveness*, the experience could have been a trauma for him rather than a beautiful learning experience.

Caring for ourselves at different ages helps us receive the nourishment we may not have had as kids. It allows us to re-parent our younger selves, so they don't go lashing out in board meetings or at the poor customer service clerk. After our little ones are integrated, we can express a more balanced range of emotions as adults. It gives us the toolbox to emotionally regulate, which means, when our inner eight-year-old wants a pint of ice cream after a really stressful day, we can lovingly care for them in a way that suits their best interest—and heal.

Bonding with our inner children gives us the opportunity to understand ourselves better and to consider the past with compassion. We can forgive our parents, and our younger selves, and see our present reality with fresh eyes.

Forgiving myself for my journey with my body has been key to my recovery—forgiving myself for every food I've ever shame-shoveled down my throat, for all the nights I did not wholly enjoy sex because of insecurity about my belly, for all the years I over-exercised my natural curves away, *I forgive myself.* I grieve those lost moments in my heart. I can't call them back. But I can live presently.

I recognize what I hope my clients will adopt: I did the best that I could. My obsession about my body and controlling my food intake were the only tools I had that helped me deal with life's challenges. Some of that was because of society; some of that was because of nurture. But after I recognized I had access to better tools, it became my responsibility to choose them.

Telling our stories makes us healers. It also makes us free. I personally feel better knowing my experiences are helping people learn the art of self-acceptance. I do this work for them and for younger Marla, who still occasionally makes an appearance. And in the name of compassion: compassion for my past; compassion for every woman who struggles with shame; and compassion to unlock the years of pain in all of us.

It is with determined patience, that I implore you to forgive yourself so that you might discover the brilliant woman inside you who is dying to live.

3

Be Your Own Best Friend

"It's not how much we give but how much
love we put into giving."
– *Mother Theresa*

On any given day, I meditate, exercise, drop my 10-year-old son Aspen off at school, provide two Reiki sessions, coach three clients, make an errand list, then run said errands. I lug in the groceries while the laundry dries. I fold the laundry while waiting on the maintenance man who is always late. By the afternoon, I'm exhausted. I'd nap, but by then it's time to collect Aspen and take him to soccer, prepare dinner, clean up the house, and *hopefully* fit in a short walk or a few texts to my girlfriends before my husband, Olaf, gets home. As I wash dishes after dinner, I am acutely aware that no one notices. In fact, Olaf mentions that I didn't take the garbage out as promised.

I hold my tongue and breathe. Moments like this make me feel unseen and unappreciated, but I know it's not *really* about him. He is an excellent partner and papa. He always shows up for our family.

This is about me, and I know it. It's my lengthy to-do list, and the unrealistic expectations I put on myself. I show up fully and do everything for everyone, taking little time to breathe. Though I strive to balance life to the best of my ability, I become overwhelmed, then self-care becomes another tiring task. By the time I get to my bath bomb, I'm so frazzled and worn out, I wilt in the tub, alleviating feelings of resentment, craving external validation, letting my tears flow.

In these moments, I'd give anything for someone to say, "Wow, Marla! I see you. You are doing a fantastic job." Instead of communicating my need for affirmation, no one knows I need consoling. They quietly observe me doing my own thing or are too preoccupied with their own lives to notice mine. I get angry and even sometimes passive-aggressive if I allow the cycle to go on for too long.

I think to myself, *Why can't Olaf see I am doing the best I can, instead of commenting on a slight shortcoming? I know . . . I made another mistake! I dropped the arugula on the ground. I forgot to buy trash bags for the second time. Why can't my mentor commend me for doing it right, as opposed to continually finding ways for me to improve? Why does Aspen get annoyed at me when I'm the one who rushes him everywhere, snacks in tow, with a Plan B outfit and his Pokémon ready? Who notices me?*

This reeling stirs frustration and sadness that rolls into an anxious ball in my belly. Then, I feel compelled to turn myself against everyone and everything outside myself. Inevitably, my shutting everyone out continues the cycle and keeps me from receiving the approval I so desperately crave.

I get snippy with my son, short with my husband, and irritated with my bestie who *never calls me first!* I know I'm not alone in this, and I've come to realize when I need the encouragement and boost that I am demanding from others, the quickest way to feel better is to give it to myself.

What? How can we be expected to fill our own cup when we've been pouring into others all day long? Easily. We take deliberate time to build ourselves up from the moment our feet hit the floor in the morning.

Marla, you're doing great. I see you making changes and doing your best. You meditated today—great job! That was a phenomenal presentation; you really blew them away. Need a second to catch your breath? I've got your back. Always. Hey, God help me out today. I am gonna need it.

I work with clients who ask me how to better their lives, how to step into their calling, embrace their bodies, and thrive. My field research as a woman, teacher, and cheerleader is sustained by one thing, and one thing only: I am my own best friend.

When I tune into the words of my higher self, I am unstoppable. If I am headed out to a speaking gig with my hair and makeup done, dressed fabulously, I first tell myself, *Great dress! Your hair looks nice! Your lipstick is gorgeous!* Because I have built a reservoir of trust with myself, I get the same boost as if someone else was saying it.

The longer I've worked in the public eye, the more important inner dialogue has become. After all, everyone will form their opinion about me, and their thoughts are not always constructive. My self-esteem is bolstered by my ability to be compassionate, affirming, and friendly toward myself—continually, not just as a short morning routine. I often see affirmations promoted as a practice for well-being, and while it is beneficial for a shift in mood, I have found slowing down and asking myself what I need to hear throughout the day is the key to taking care of myself.

After sharing an anti-weight loss post that triggered many women to send me multiple private messages, informing me that they are happy to be selling weight loss supplements and lucky to finally lose the weight—I needed some extra TLC. I was aiming to be praised for my great idea; instead, most of the messages were an unkind attempt to put me in my place.

So, I took some space. I put one hand on my heart and one on my belly, I hugged myself, rocked myself, and said words of support that felt good to me. Then, I stayed in that feeling until I experienced a sense of fulfillment. As I came down, epiphanies surfaced.

See? You didn't need all that external validation. I know you're trying so hard to be a great service to women, friend, loving mom, and wife—but the recognition you needed most was here all along.

Relaxing into this state always brings me back into the present. Then, I can be fully available—to myself, and inadvertently to my husband

and son. It's an entirely different headspace than running around like my hair is on fire all day (a concept made even more absurd when I consider the fact that most of my to-do list is inauthentic).

Olaf used to say to me, "You are stressing yourself out about entertainment. If going to the beach or meeting a friend is causing stress, maybe it isn't worth it."

This made me realize that my *go go go!* mentality was showing up in all my *fun* moments too. In turn, I started asking myself, *Do I really want to live like a crazy woman with a hot flame under my booty?*

I mean, come on. Look at your life. How many details are just superfluous things you'd probably forget about if you weren't determined to drive yourself crazy? What would your day look like if you felt like you didn't have to do the things you're supposed to do?

Many people push themselves over the top with obligations because they fear the judgment of others. I wish I could say I don't relate, but the reality is—we all fall subject to it. Be-Friending myself means giving myself permission to stop caring about what others think, and only listening to my own guidance. Be-Friending myself means knowing my stopping point and putting limits on what is possible for me to do in one day. Be-Friending myself means asking my *body* for the truth—rather than my mind that always wants to do *more*.

My client, Gail, was exhausted by being everything to everyone. She had a huge community that relied on her for mentoring, emotional support, and practical needs. She took this obligation seriously because she wanted to be of service. But this desire to help had begun to make her tired, sick, and deflated. Gail didn't know how to say *no*. She decided to test out speaking *No!* every time she felt herself people-pleasing or taking action because she feared she'd hurt someone's feelings. Gail reported that it was scary to deny others at first.

"Holy moly, Marla. I thought I would cave when I told my friend I couldn't pick her son up from school. There was an awkward silence on the phone, and my friend didn't know how to respond. The thing is, I would normally stop everything to help a friend, but inevitably my whole day gets derailed. Then, I feel like a victim to everyone else's needs. But before I called her, I realized—I am in control here. I can say *no*."

Gail felt her family was the most challenging because she loved them and didn't want to let them down. When she realized that repressing her anger doesn't help anyone, she leaned into her boundaries even more. By saying "yes," when she meant "no," she was living a lie.

What surprised Gail was how her desire to please was directly related to her body. She thought that she had to be ultra-thin to be loved. She was an over-exerciser and bulimic who wanted her body to look perfect. Gail went to the gym every day, convinced she wouldn't find a husband unless her butt was tight. Gail hung out with friends who valued diets and cleanses and shunned anything with sugar. After getting married and having kids, her life was still suffering. That's why she contacted me—to guide her into letting go of these behaviors.

What Gail didn't realize was that the act of wanting attention for her body came from a more profound fear that she wasn't good enough. This belief showed up not only in her preoccupation with her physical appearance but in her people-pleasing.

As we peeled back the layers, Gail came to realize these patterns had been carried out since she was very young, and she was hopeful to break the cycle by uprooting the negative belief.

Together, we dove into healing the need to be perfect, replacing it with the challenge to live authentically. Within weeks, Gail saw improvement in her confidence, and her personal relationships. Her soul-searching helped heal her mind, and as a byproduct, the symptoms of bulimia healed incrementally—as she leaned into truth. Gail became her own best friend throughout the process, making her time outside of coaching less lonely. She concluded, *I, Gail, am beautiful and worthy of love regardless of what I look like, or what I do or don't do for others.* Talk about a profound realization!

Now, don't get me wrong. I am certain my calling in life is to serve others with the things that I have learned. I love building women up, being a sounding board, and pointing them back toward themselves. But all these things are pointless if I am out of alignment with myself, or if I am doing them for the wrong reasons. There are infinite ways we can be of service. But if we are doing it to create worthiness, we need to take a more in-depth look at ourselves.

So, you want to lose weight? I ask my clients.

Ideas surrounding weight loss always make me raise my eyebrow, even for my seemingly "healthy" clients, who insist they want to lose fifty pounds as an act of *love* toward their bodies. While this is closer to what I am hoping to hear, the reality is—when we love our bodies, we do not command, *we listen.*

For those who are emotionally eating and binge eating, you want to lose weight. You are aware that your weight isn't authentic. It is a result of unhealthy behaviors. However, the general rule of thumb I see is that clients who desire weight loss inherently have that goal because of external influences. They think that losing weight means they are healed.

We typically find it's never about the number on the scale . . . it's always about a negative belief or behavior that needs to be mined. Once they let go of society's values, they can access a deeper self-love and enjoy friendship with themselves.

Love your Body, Love Yourself can be especially triggering for this group, because they want to get thin, *then* love themselves. But truth be told, we must love ourselves first—*Don't blame me. I don't make the rules; I just teach them!* I have found it fundamentally impossible to will self-love. It doesn't work that way. Moreover, it's a false sense of security and grappling for control. I've lived it over and over again. When my weight would drop for a few weeks, I felt sexy and excited. *Woohoo! I've made it. I can finally wear my short shorts and let my hips swagger. I have permission to fully live my life!*

Then a girls' trip would come, or a wedding, or any holiday that invites a cheese tray and wine, and I'd be triggered out of enjoying myself. I'd either compulsively eat treats—not even enjoying them or count every calorie—making myself and everyone miserable around me. I could never escape the fear, *What if I gained it all back?*

As a result, I could never be present with anyone, except the bully in my head. And who would want to hang out with *that* girl? We all know her: she's that critical, impatient family member or acquaintance everyone cringes around because she's always making harsh comments and wielding judgments on others; she's the girl you're dying to escape from because she sucks up all the oxygen in the room. She's mean. And I was mean—to myself.

Until I learned how to create *real* security within myself, and realized my weight has nothing to do with my worth as a woman. As a result, I started to create security for myself by cleaning my life up in other ways. I stopped beating myself up, quit overexercising, and created space to truly connect with Marla—entertaining her ideas, indulging in her desires, and cultivating her dreams. Talk about a bestie!

It helped me determine my *why*. When I finally slowed down, I could truly ask myself, *Am I exercising, dieting, and cleansing because it feels healthy and good for me? Or is this coming from a place of fear and validation-seeking?*

The truths I had to sit with were loud and uncomfortable, as most pivotal truths are. I was shocked to realize that most of my actions were fueled by beliefs I'd never subscribed to—from societal to familial—and I had some choices to make. Once I took my power back, I started to contemplate what life would be like if I only did actions that felt good. *Holy moly!* The concept felt wild and scary. Until I leaned in.

When I stepped out of overexercising and a life of restriction, I felt unsteady at first, sure. But I also felt a tremendous, all-encompassing relief. No longer chronically beating myself up, I was able to focus on things I actually enjoyed, and *indulge* in healthy foods and exercise for the right reasons. My to-do lists became shorter and were broken up with periods of decompression and delicious afternoon naps on the back porch. Additionally, my relationship with social media began to change. I started pursuing in-person connection more than online communication; I stopped depending on the likes of a photograph to make me feel good about myself; and I stopped comparing myself to the thousands of Instagram accounts with the perfect bodies and latest diet hacks. I settled into myself, and my life flourished.

What I share to my coaching clients underscored itself to me:

When you become your best friend, you will love yourself, and when you love yourself, the body you want will be the body you have.

Then, everything falls into place, because you are finally free and encouraged to be exactly who you were made to be. As a result, your body will shift to match the state of your confidence level until the outside matches the inside—*beautifully.*

If you want to learn how to have more feelings of positivity and become a better friend to yourself, check out my FREE "Body-Love Meditation," https://loveyourbodyloveyourself.com/body-love.6

---

6   Marla Mervis-Hartmann, "Breaking the Cycle of Emotional Eating," *Love Your Body Love Yourself,* https://loveyourbodyloveyourself.com/body-love.

4

Be "Bad"

"We all have a hungry heart, and one of the things
we hunger for is happiness."
– *Mary Oliver*

You can't mess it up!" I told Sarah. There's no *bad* choice when it comes to your dinner. She was practically pleading for me to shame her for eating french fries instead of ordering a salad. She begged again for a regimen or a food plan. *Nope! It's not happening.* The only suggestion I gave her was to eat food that made her feel good. If on Saturday, a big piece of chocolate cake feels shameful, then don't eat it. But if on Sunday she felt the internal green light, and it felt pleasurable, absolutely enjoy. The only *unhelpful* choice we can make about food is eating things that make us feel bad about ourselves; in a perfect world, food would never be given that much power over us. The point is to examine the beliefs behind our opinions about sustenance. When we believe the lies that we are *good* or *bad*, we categorize food as *right* or *wrong*, which ultimately sets us up for a lifestyle of restriction, and unintentionally—failure.

Food is neutral. And the key to seeing it correctly is repairing our relationship with ourselves. I asked Sarah why she ate the french fries if she knew they were *bad*. She said she was exhausted by her own rules and needed a break. Exactly. Had she been living a life of intuitive indulgence, and not feeling deprived, she wouldn't have felt exhausted. Then she could have chosen the fries out of liberation, and most likely wouldn't have given it a second thought after.

Years later, Sarah told me that the conversation about the french fries freed her. She didn't realize how much stress she caused herself by shame spiraling after indulging in something entirely reasonable. Her newfound sovereignty led her to make authentic choices because she wanted to. Not because she *should*.

Sometimes, it's actually about eating more. My clients are often shocked to hear this, but the reality is—*health* is multifaceted. It's not always about weight. My thyroid and adrenal issues, for example, have been challenging aspects of my health. When I first received support from a doctor, she had me write down my food. To share my food choices with another human being felt more vulnerable than mooning my whole high school. It felt terrifying to share what and how much I consumed.

I was confident my doctor would shun me for my *bad* choices, and the gluttonous amount of food that I ate. But being a concerned patient, and a good student, I shared honestly. I documented every food, even when I was the most ashamed. After turning it over to her, I was surprised to hear her exclaim, "You aren't eating enough, and the quality of your food has no nutrition or sustenance. No wonder your health is suffering, and you are hungry all the time. You need to eat more!"

What? I thought. I could not believe it.

It was that experience that made me rethink my obsession with food. I blamed myself for thinking about calories all the time. I referred to myself as a food addict because it was on my mind 24-7. My body kept telling me to eat, but I would deny myself, because I was rationing out every meal. Then I would be shocked to find I was thinking about food between meals because my body was not getting proper nourishment. Go figure.

I began to wonder, *Why is our relationship to food so painful?* As I considered the question in my life, and in the lives of my students, I reduced it down to one thing—shame. Shame is what makes feeding our bodies, something we should be able to do naturally and without fear, tremendously complicated. *Doesn't that seem outrageous?*

Shame creates irrational fears, and mental distortions around food—even when it's healthy! Some diets claim black beans are bad; whole wheat bread is out; grapes are too sugary; no potatoes—at all, even nutrient-dense sweet potatoes. *What?* That sounds absurd to me. And yet, I participated in it willingly. I fully believed if I ate the right proportions, I could diminish cravings for carbohydrates and sugar and have full control. I told myself once I was the perfect weight, then I would love myself. Talk about malnourishment. I was robbing myself of the mental and emotional support I needed from my truest friend–*Marla*.

I didn't realize it at the time, but my negative beliefs about food were keeping me from my own companionship, support, and love. I was a bag of bones emotionally. In turn, I knew I had to get down to the root. When I started to pull those core beliefs apart, I could see that I didn't have to give them power anymore. By replacing my beliefs, I could let go of pain and allow myself peace around my choices.

Some examples of my negative beliefs around food included:

If I overeat chocolate, then I'm a failure.

If I go for seconds, then I have no control.

If I eat a bag of potato chips, that means I'm a loser.

Fill in your own *if* statement. Then, let's take a closer look together!

Hear me when I say, you may not feel great about yourself, but it doesn't mean that you're a failure, loser, or are out of control. Stop making it personal. It's food. It'll digest, and be a thing of the past.

Sometimes we need a wake-up call. Including me. Luckily, I keep showing up as my best friend. I have myself to rely on when I need a boost. I counter the pressure society places on diets and body image with solid rationale and vibrant play—anything to help myself out of a funk!

Through the following questions, I was able to identify where my self-worth was connected to food. I invite you to do the same.

What are my beliefs about food?

What are some of the ways pain shows up in my relationship with food?

How do I look at food and my self-worth?

How am I setting myself up for more pain in my life?

When I addressed the pain that is present with food, it helped me determine what out-of-alignment beliefs I had around feeding myself. I also noticed which food choices created the strongest emotional reactions in me. For example:

My belief: *I have no control when eating chocolate cake because it tastes so good.*

While I love chocolate cake, the statement itself is illogical. So, I took a closer look at my thought loop beyond the belief:

I am obsessed with chocolate. I wonder how much I can eat and still be thin. Maybe two pieces, or three, if I get an extra HIIT (High Intensity Interval Training) routine tomorrow at the gym? But what about all the sugar? Sugar is bad; everyone knows that. What is Allison going to think of me if she sees me eating it? I won't eat any dinner and go for it. It is so good. I hope I can stop eating it. Shit. I'll probably overeat and make myself sick. I am eating it anyway. I don't care. I'll eat it.

It's amazing how one piece of cake could make me completely lose my sanity. The anxiety and negativity consumed me. By the time I took my first bite, I wasn't even present or available to enjoy it. I wasn't in my body. I was panic-stricken. I would eat it as quickly as possible to get the whole experience over with. I didn't know how to love food, because I didn't know how to BE-Friend myself. As a byproduct of my own anxiety and guilt, I'd comfort myself with a second piece just to self-soothe. I'd self-abandon and eat even more.

What did this create? Well . . . a really miserable relationship with cake.

My ultimate truth: chocolate cake equals anxiety and fear.

I am sure I'm not alone in that. In fact, I invite you to take out a journal and answer the following questions. I imagine they'll point you to a similar discovery.

What are the evident ways you're bringing conflict into your relationship with food?

Are you restricting, overeating, or micromanaging food?

Are you eating foods you're allergic to?

Are you not listening to your body?

Are you dieting, bingeing, or purging?

Do you label food as good or bad?

Take it one step further. Create your own questions. With awareness comes the power to change patterns. Love yourself enough to dive deep.

I repeat—diets don't work! Dieting can create insanity around our food. The reason the diet industry is a $70 billion industry is that they keep selling us the next new fad. We tell ourselves; *this diet is going to work this time. I got it all figured out. My determination will make it happen. Stand back, world. Get ready, because this diet is my passport to weight loss and ultimate happiness.* Except it isn't. It's a rude awakening, I know.

When we buy into this delusion, we commit to the emotional rollercoaster, then end up eventually gaining the weight back—and then some, while compromising our sanity. For some reason, we place shame upon ourselves, thinking that we're not doing it *right*. We believe we can't get it together; that there's ultimately something wrong with us. We worship others who have had quick, temporary, success and ask them how they lost weight. I am not sure why we don't see through the insanity, but diet culture is insidious.

Though we may get a high from restricting food, especially when we start seeing the number decrease on the scale, the low that follows can be equally as powerful and crippling. The more weight we lose, the more challenging it becomes to shed the pounds, so we restrict ourselves more. As we white-knuckle food with a *no pain, no gain* mentality, we create a life that is unsustainable. Despite our enthusiasm, that usually devolves into panic-stricken mania, our systems cannot be tricked. Our bodies go into deprivation mode, thinking, *This woman is crazy! I'm not getting any food! I've gotta talk some sense into her! Sound the alarm for delicious, fatty foods!*

Emotions soar. Stress happens. Then we find ourselves in the middle of the night, pawing around the pantry, scavenging for empty carbohydrates. By morning, shame floods the open channel, and catapults us into another round of dieting that recreates the cycle.

It never stops.

In the book, *Intuitive Eating, A Revolutionary Anti-Diet Approach*, Evelyn Tribole and Elyse Resch note:

"Dieting is a form of short-term starvation. Consequently, when you are given the first opportunity to really eat, eating is often experienced at such an intensity that it feels uncontrollable, a desperate act. In the moment of biological hunger, all intentions to stick with the food plan are fleeting and paradoxically irrelevant.[7]

I adore this book because it gives scientific information coupled with practical application to regain our sovereignty around food. The authors address how our society has emphasized dieting so much that the only way to regain sanity is to return to oneself. Dieting is a lost cause and a sad one. To make matters worse, their research shows that 90 percent of people who go on a diet will gain the weight back, meaning a further blow to their confidence and self-esteem.

So, how do we approach this conundrum of misinformation on physical health?

The answer is both simple and triggering. We surrender. If you can get past the latter part, you'll find the resolve of letting go defuses the pain of holding on. By listening to what our body wants, we can begin to trust ourselves—we build trust with our best friend. Is there any greater reward?

Finally, don't you, as a self-respecting person, deserve a say at this point? How many years have you been on the earth? How many of those years have you been deeply in tune with your favorite foods? Do you acknowledge when you're hungry or full? What are you truly craving? Wouldn't it be a beautiful journey to discover these things? Doesn't your best friend deserve that?

---

7   Evelyn Tribole and Elyse Resch, *Intuitive Eating, A Revolutionary Anti-Diet Approach (New York: St. Martin's Essentials, 2020).*

Okay, I admit it, this isn't something that happens overnight. In fact, I would invite you to bring someone alongside you on this journey who is *even more* compassionate than your friendliest inner voice—consider a bestie, a guide, or a therapist! Our goal is to flood ourselves with love and release the rest. We must let go of diet mentality and the voices in our head that reinforce limitations. When we do this, we learn to tune into, and honor our intuition.

When we're controlling ourselves consistently, we get out of alignment with what our body wants and needs, and trust is lost. By getting quiet and listening, we may hear our truth differently—without the voice of shame eclipsing our own, eating becomes natural. Then our dialogue sounds a little more rational: *Oh, wow! My body doesn't even want the extra cookie or feels comfortable with the ice cream sundae I ate.*

When we allow ourselves a moment to check in with what our body wants, we have the opportunity to feel encouraged when we desire what we actually *need*. Have you ever just craved a salad? Fresh blueberries? A mouthwatering fillet of fresh salmon? If your answer is no, consider this might be because you have labeled these options, *diet food*. What a bummer! These nutrient-dense foods can be a party! Fresh strawberries with a scoop of cream, anyone? A delicious bar of dark chocolate? A savory dish of seasoned brussels sprouts? Yum!

By giving ourselves permission to enjoy all food, we might come to find we naturally gravitate toward the things that we once considered *boring*. This radical act of listening is a bold act of love in that it's giving ourselves a clean slate, to start again, to rendezvous with food in a new way. And if you can't give yourself that permission, if you still feel like you need it from the outside world, well you're in luck. I happen to be right here, opening the door for you.

Madame, you're allowed to be the one at the table who mindfully chooses a cheeseburger when everyone else is eating salad. Likewise, you're allowed to be the one at the table who mindfully chooses a vegetarian dish when everyone else is eating steak. Have you caught on yet? What I'm saying is, you can eat whatever the hell you want, because you have the power, and I want you to stand in it, despite criticism from naysayers—whether they are family or friends.

Soon enough you'll be tuning in before you make selections. Your confidence will skyrocket and will take the place of the negative emotions that previously dictated all of your choices. You will achieve serenity with food—finally. You will feel empowered to indulge in the foods that you've for so long been deprived. Extra cheese; maple syrup; maybe some fresh cherries on the side! Enjoy it as you embrace the sheer pleasure of "being bad."

5

Be Still

"Be still and know that I am God."
– *Psalm 46:10*

Jordan was livid with her partner. Once again, the floors were covered in crud, and she didn't even notice, let alone lift a finger. This was their chronic argument: one of those fights that pointed to the issue beyond the issue.

How many times have I hounded her about this? she thought. *Please don't make me out to be the bad one!*

"I'll help you if you ask," her partner said, nonchalantly. This sent Jordan fuming. She threw her hands in the air and let out a guttural, infuriated groan.

"Urrrrrrgh! You'll help? How did this become my job, that you only help with? We're a team!" Jordan retreated from the argument, furious.

Why couldn't she just notice it needed to get done and take some pride in their home? Why did this argument always have to get loud and mean?

Not even an evening soak could help Jordan unwind. She begrudgingly put on her pj's, and went to bed early—irritated in the space between asleep and awake, until 3:00 a.m. rolled around, and she was wide-eyed. Jordan never knew what to do with her rage. She turned over, seething at her partner, who slept comfortably next to her, then got out of bed.

Making little effort to stay quiet, she made her way to the fridge for a late-night raid to eat all the leftover garlic bread. Even though she wasn't hungry. Even though it hadn't been all that tasty at dinner. Even though bread wasn't even what she was craving. Just because. She caved to filling the empty hole inside her heart with a carb binge, and went to bed afterward with bad breath, negative feelings about herself, and heartburn.

Jordan's method of help really didn't *help*. It just made matters worse.

Well, that didn't save the day. I didn't even want to eat that bread, she shamefully thought to herself.

What do we do when we don't want to use food as our coping mechanism? What do we do when food is no longer our savior? What do we do when we are no longer *craving the craving*? Is it possible we are looking for an answer that isn't edible? I know so.

When we're starting to find relief and a new relationship with food, there will be moments of: *I don't even want to . . .*

eat this bag of chips.
reach for that bag of chocolates.
obsess about my body.
research another diet.
do another 30-day plan.

When this happens, it begs the question, *Now what?* And without fielding that question thoroughly, we can be thrust into autopilot, where our old behaviors kick in and hijack our better judgment. This usually works to our detriment. It can look like reaching for that cookie we don't actually want, after the brownie we didn't "need." It can look like indulging in a cheese plate knowing dairy wreaks havoc on our body. It can look like succumbing to our monkey-mind that loves to take over and invite undue amounts of stress into our lives before we even realize what's happening.

I advise my clients to develop a plan for when they face the *Now what?* experience.

What steps can we take when we don't want to choose food as our coping mechanism or to binge eat anymore; when we genuinely want to make healthier choices but feel confined to our learned behaviors?

Genie had the same questions for me. She came in feeling entirely self-defeated by her bingeing and restriction patterns.

"Marla, I hadn't binged in weeks," she began, "then I saw my ex-boyfriend. I came home and involuntarily went through the motions of preparing my food for a binge. It's like my self-respect went out the window. I didn't want to do it, but I wasn't in my right mind. I felt completely disconnected from my body and my progress. I was devastated after, because I truly thought this behavior was gone."

Suffice it to say, Genie was caught off guard. Understandably so. I mean what's more triggering than an ex-boyfriend? Not much. This is a common pitfall when we are recovering, when something terrible, we'll call it *Ben*, creeps in. In turn, we are thrust into a mindset of all-out warfare.

The worst part? When we are weakened by emotional overwhelm, we too easily sabotage all our most valuable efforts by shuttling to the closest sub sandwich bar. Sixteen meatballs later, we find ourselves sweaty and full of bread—not the ideal place to access the self-compassion we so desperately need.

After Genie calmed down, I encouraged her to acknowledge that although she *did* binge, she didn't have the emotional commitment nor the need to continue bingeing. I coached her to see the behavior was no longer serving her. Together, we were able to determine a better way to mitigate the emotional flood brought on by *Ben*. I encouraged her to be patient with herself—patience throughout the process is key.

Furthermore, most do not jump from regular, emotional eating, or turmoil with food, to a place of immediate peace. Healing is not a linear process. It has layers, dips, plateaus, and yes—peaks. But every point of the process is worth celebrating, so I urge my clients to identify their wins.

I know many coaches promise instant results. I am honest—so I am not one of them. In my own experience and with my clients—I revel in peeling back the onion. Moreover, I believe discomfort can be a profound teacher that brings us into the present, where we can navigate *now what?* experiences in a way that truly serves us.

Many times when I thought my belly was hungry, it was because my soul was starving. While I was standing naked in front of my bathroom mirror as negativity swirled through my head, my narrative sounded something like *You look disgusting. I can't believe that's what you look like. You will never control your food long enough to be thin.*

I heard a gentle, strong silence on the other side of my distress telling me to *Be still. Be still* in my thoughts. *Be still* in my criticisms. *Be still* in my quickness to self-harm. It's a comfort for me to believe there is a source of love higher than myself that is looking out for me.

On more occasions than one, I have found myself pouring my heart out in prayer, confident I was being heard. This strengthened my *belief* that I could overcome my demons by allowing the void inside myself to be filled with *love* instead of food.

This belief that I belonged to something led me out of overeating, under nourishing, and ruthlessly controlling my diet. When I was left with no other answer, I was invited into a place of surrender that changed everything for good.

When I slow down, I hear God; when I'm running around at an unsustainable pace—all divinity gets drowned out by my own chaos and noise. I remember one particular afternoon during my acting career, after receiving my third audition rejection, I was pacing around anxiously in my small Queens apartment. I didn't know what to do with the rush of emotions pulsing through me. I only knew that food would curb the emotion. As I raced to the kitchen, I was irritated to find my refrigerator was empty of any sugary substance to relieve my pain. Maybe it was a gift because I was forced to sit with my own pain. So, I did what any bright, young, twenty-something would do: I fell on my floor and cried. *And cried.* Until finally, I felt a rush of warmth and the sensation of being held. I heard a faint voice that softly said, "It's okay. You are loved. You are loved."

Relief came by choosing—well, being forced—to *feel.* It was a divine breaking point, where there was nothing to hide me from God's assuring message that some dumb audition could never determine my worth. It was a good reminder that I have a greater something advocating for me when I struggle with having my own back: a higher love that *I* *need*. I took this experience into my next audition and there was a level of confidence that I never experienced before. I felt valuable, creative, vibrant, expressive and free. My detachment from the *result*, and focus on the fact that I am divine, made me shine—because I was aligned with my higher self and my higher power. Moving forward, I noticed the more connected I was to my worth, the better I performed.

I've never really been the type to go solo. I'm only human, after all. I don't always know my highest good—though I'd love to believe I do. I couldn't make the insanity go away on my own. At some point, I recognized I had to ask for relief from the shame that was eroding my life from the inside out. Before I could love myself, I had to *learn* what unconditional love looked like.

I let God love me when I could not accept myself. I thought I was looking for relief that only a chocolate cookie or a smaller number on the scale could provide. But that never worked. I needed unconditional love expressed to every part of me: my brokenness, my exhaustion, and my shame. By surrendering to God's love, I have allowed myself to feel worthy, supported, and accepted. This gave me the ultimate guide to navigating pain, as the comfort I continually receive surpasses any other.

Not only has my spiritual connection redeemed me from every seemingly hopeless circumstance, but it is also something that is always available for me; it doesn't require a frantic outcry of hopelessness to show up. It just *is*; it provides a consistent, specific nourishment that I need. Prayer works for me.

When we lose connection to ourselves on a spiritual level, food, body obsession, and other addictions can fill the empty space. The painful void inside us craves connection, craves attention, craves spiritual food. No amount of weight loss or peanut butter fudge ice cream will fill it—I know, I've tried. Only a deep connection to *love* is the answer. *Love* taught me I could not only heal my relationship with food but also flourish past it.

One of my clients, Jocelyn, was kicked out of the house by her drug-addicted mother at the age of fourteen. Left to fend for herself in survival mode, she found an apartment, lied about her age to sign for it, and got a job as a waitress. She was a fighter; she was not going to give up on herself. But she was not without vices.

At night, binge eating became Jocelyn's savior. She'd numb herself from feelings of loneliness with whatever was left in the fridge. She'd usually go to bed full, miserable, and just as sad as she'd felt prior to binging.

"I know it might sound crazy, Marla, but I believe God led me to you so that I could heal . . ." Jocelyn said. She was ready to end her toxic relationship with her body and food. Through our work together, she stopped binge eating, and learned how to satiate her true needs. The vacancy her mother left was significant. Prior to our work together, she'd stay in bed for days and sabotage her self-care efforts. Together, we realized that she didn't want to fight or hustle anymore. Jocelyn was tired of striving—she just wanted to be loved.

Through inner child work and inviting the undying love of her higher power to fill her cup, Jocelyn stopped binge eating and created a spiritual, self-care practice. Her capacity to receive and give love has now surpassed anything she had ever experienced growing up.

If you were not given the love you needed as a child, finding love from a compassionate higher power is the answer.

It's okay if you don't know how to search for a higher power. God is always pursuing us. Don't resist God because of your emotional state; you don't have to have peace to be worthy of love. Let God find you in whatever state you are in. Whether we are lost, or deliberately running, or pissed off—*all* of these things are okay; all are part of being in a relationship. In fact, they are pretty authentic to the lateral relationships in our lives because vulnerability is hard; still—God wants us, pursues us, and desires balance for this.

I am the most certain of this because I believe *balance* is the signature of everything divine. The same power that creates waves in the ocean, clouds in the sky, and balance in nature created you. The universe provides order naturally, when we allow it, *if* we allow it. When we search for Spirit, Spirit will find us. I've seen it too many times for it not to be true.

For example, my dearest friend, Rachel, had an ongoing, painful relationship with God. She didn't trust that her higher power would support her. She lost her dad early in life to cancer, and she was devastated. When her mom finally did remarry, Rachel finally had the father figure that she had always longed for.

Years later, her stepdad died suddenly in a car accident. From that point on, she believed that God hated her and went as far away from spirituality and religion as possible. And yet, she shared with me, "Marla, I have been doing everything I can to shut God out. And yet, I feel like I have angels all around me. People holding my pain and giving me love, random acts of kindness that hit me so close to home that my heart has blasted open.

"On a hike, I found myself in a clearing that was still. I screamed and yelled at God, 'If you loved me, you wouldn't have taken my dads away. I hate you!' After this rant, I felt a peace that I never felt before. Strangely, I felt heard and cared for.

"Then, seemingly divinely, in that moment, a deer came close to me and stared—as if to say, *You are not alone.* That experience made me know I needed God more than ever to deal with my pain."

I know it isn't easy for some of us to let God in. Social and familial trauma can occur that makes it even more challenging. And so in these cases, we tread lightly. We gently open up to the power of love. We look and allow love to heal us. Love is the neutral power that never ceases.

And so, I pose this question, *Can you allow yourself to be full of something else? Will you?*

When we begin to fill that empty, angry or sad space with more connection to self and God, we unlock abundant access to healing. And no, that healing won't always feel great, but we will at least have peace as we work through our pain.

The pain of acting out with food is familiar and comforting. We know how to operate from the known behavior: restriction, dieting, binge eating, shame talk, etcetera. The unknown can feel terrifying. Change is not our strong suit as human beings. We know what life looks like when we continue to feel, react, and behave the same way.

Because we are creatures of habit, even the goals we aggressively set for ourselves can be thrown to the wayside time and again because the fear of the unknown draws us back to familiar habits. The mystery can be daunting if we don't know how to change our perspective. I have found the most brilliant shifts in perspectives come when I consider if something *might* be true.

Can you consider you might be loved? Can you check it out?

After a frustrating time helping my son with his schoolwork, I could feel the agitation growing in me. I tossed the pencil I was holding across the counter, then moved around the kitchen, like a lion, ready to pounce. When I found my chocolate stash, I closed my eyes for a moment, and heard the words, *Be still.* My hands clutched the rustling bag as I thought, *I don't have to eat this.* And that moment—was a breakthrough.

I put the chocolate out of my sight and reach, so I didn't compulsively shove it in my mouth and shamefully repeat the past, and I allowed the commanding feelings of pain to overcome me. When they did, they were relentless. I felt like I was coming out of my skin. I breathed deep, recognized my own racing heartbeat, and told myself I was strong enough to *feel* and not eat. To *be still*, and not eat.

Soon, the pain released me. And I sighed at the grace I felt.

You've got this Marla, see? It's not scary.

This intentional connection took me less than a minute and resulted in a pivotal moment that rewrote my future with food. When we rewire our nervous system's response to feelings and sit in discomfort, we say *yes* to more expansion and freedom with ourselves and with God.

In my Pleasure Plan group program, one woman had an epiphany that if she was sad, angry, and upset, she didn't have to eat over it.

She said, "I can want to binge and not do it."

I could hear the hope in her voice when she spoke, as she talked about waiting for the desire to binge to go away. I encouraged her. The urge would take time, but it would fade.

As Glennon Doyle puts it, "Feelings are for feeling."[8]

Happiness is not the only feeling that is allowed. The more we can sit and *be* in our own void with scary emotions, the better. We are stronger than we think. Suffering is inevitable, but pain passes. On the other side of our immediate feeling is another feeling—it's in our power to honor it by allowing it *to be*.

---

8   Doyle, Glennon. *Untamed*. New York: The Dial Press, 2020.

6

Be Listening

"And I said to my body, softly, 'I want to be your friend.' It took a long breath. And replied, 'I have been waiting my whole life for this.'"
—*Nayyirah Waheed*

With my head stuck to the pillow, my mind was racing with all the things on my to-do list. The rest of the day was already consumed, and my feet hadn't even hit the floor. *Get up!* I commanded myself. But my heavy body wasn't going anywhere. Just days before, I couldn't slow down or even fall asleep. No amount of meditation and Reiki could stop my mind. I was continually stressed and agitated. Only later would I learn that my thyroid was striving so hard to function properly.

As a Reiki Master who couldn't soothe herself, I felt like a fraud. I was tired and wired, raging with shame. Body shame not only happens when we don't like our appearance, but also when we experience chronic pain and illness. We can grow impatient, upset, and angry at our bodies for being sick or hurt. Ever experience a small injury at the gym during a workout class that you just didn't obey? Only to find the more pressure you put on that weak foot the longer it took to feel *just right* again? Drained energy sources in the body due to overuse and a disregard of physical exhaustion.

Western culture doesn't prioritize rest; as a result, the body tallies our poor discernment and rebels at the eleventh hour, usually during our most important moments. Have you ever been excited about going on vacation, only to end up sicker than a dog in the hotel resort while your family is at the beach? That could leave anyone angry at their bodies. *When do I get a break?* we say, begrudgingly, as though we weren't the ones actively neglecting ourselves. *When we give ourselves one,* I tell my clients.

Slowing down is considered a luxury not an imperative. Lucy was strung out on life. She came to me anxious, tired and overwhelmed. She could barely sit still through our sessions.

She complained of insomnia, binge eating and losing her hair.

"Why can't I just calm down? Honestly, Marla I don't even think I can. I am so tired, but my body won't let me stop."

I understood this phenomenon so deeply because of my own experience. After working together for a while, it was clear that slowing down meant danger to Lucy.

Growing up in an environment of abuse and social instability, if she slowed down, she could be a target. It took time to unwind, but together I guided Lucy back to her body to find a place that was safe enough to relax. Lucy learned how to become her own best friend by unwinding this fear in her body's timing. This became a testament of her love for herself.

The first indicator that I was not being a good friend to my body was when my thyroid started screaming at me. My body would surge with adrenaline, then crash. My adrenal glands were running a chronic relay race—all in response to my mental gymnastics, and beloved *to-dos.* This created a toxic cycle. I wanted to crack the whip on myself for not being able to get out of bed after I'd put myself in a place of debilitating exhaustion. *I have a life to lead and shit to do! People depend on me! I don't have time for this!*

So, I'd push myself, only to find I couldn't thrive in my efforts, because something as simple as walking to the kitchen exhausted me. Believing my body was holding me back, I'd self-abandon a bit more

that the universe is drawing our attention to. It can be present subtly, especially in chronic conditions. There are residual energies that build up from years of not having a good relationship with ourselves. It's up to us to work through that pain.

There are ways to do that by taking the time and having the right attitude and focus. Pain is an element that our body is holding, but it doesn't define us, nor does it have to impact our future.

For example, pushing away anger is counterproductive. It may seem to save us time in the short term, when we can't pencil in a meltdown, but having a conversation and asking, *Why are you angry, and how can I serve you?* can offer us immediate relief, as well as years free of blockage and frustration. Furthermore, pain can be a profound teacher if we are willing to slow down and learn from it. It's easy to be nasty to the body part that isn't working well. By having a kinder approach, we can have a real conversation with our bodies.

One morning after another night of insomnia due to surging adrenals, I decided to have a good ole chat with my body. I got alone, in a quiet space, and leaned in. What I learned about myself was a game changer.

As I began to connect to myself, I could identify the point of pain, which, in the moment, felt like deep heaviness. My limbs felt weighted and lethargic. I remained patient with the feelings of dread that were stored inside me. I keenly focused my breath, as my chest arose and fell. I focused on sending it to different parts of my body.

I let go of all my expectations and positioned myself as a witness. Slowly, my emotions began to surface. They were thick and fog-like—permeating every part of me. I allowed myself to respond in real time. I began to cry. Shame and anger were palpable and poured out of me. At one point, it felt excruciating, but I knew I could handle it. Strangely, I felt like I was tuning in with a friend who was having a good cry. I enjoyed being there for her. At one point, my mind tried to kick me out of the experience by distracting me with silly thoughts. I redirected them as the pain went through waves of subsiding and intensifying.

Asking questions like,

Help me understand, I'd say.
What do you need?
Where does it hurt?
How far back does it hurt?
What other memories bring up this feeling?

After my intuition began to reveal answers, it became clear, my body wasn't out to get me. My adrenals said in a quiet voice, *Why are you angry with me? I am doing the best I can. Please slow down.* I recognized that being a good friend to myself meant heeding my body's request and denying myself the temptation to rush.

This was the most intimate moment I had ever experienced with this pain. My heart opened and flooded with compassion. Big tears poured down my face. I then realized all the ways that I'd been pushing myself too hard, ignoring my needs, and scolding my body for resting. I'd been unkind to myself for so long—to become my own ally was powerful! This alleviated the notion that I was in any way defective because I started to feel better. The only thing that had ever been *wrong* with me was that I hadn't been listening for years.

I apologized to myself, rocking back and forth, and lamenting profusely. It felt like a miracle had taken place. My body began to relax. I was no longer a ball of nervous energy; I was soothed and calm. No amount of ashwagandha could have done that. Only *Marla* could have done that.

You can always talk to your body. It may feel weird, but in my experience, it works. The willingness to do something different will create new results. We don't realize we are always in conversation with ourselves—for better and for worse. Why not have conscious conversations that can restore us to peace with our bodies?

Sure, it may not mean that all of your pain will immediately disappear—but it might. In some cases, *it does.* No matter the pace, I can guarantee one thing—healing will occur.

Moment to moment, we have a choice on *how* we relate to our bodies. We can be a victim or a master to our situation. Through empathy, we show ourselves compassion, and can begin to feel healthy and awake again. If we serve our bodies, they serve us right back. Then—we don't have to self-crucify to get out of bed in the morning. We'll be ready for the day because we'll be excited about it. We owe this to ourselves.

Are you starting to pick up on the common theme? We are learning to be a good friend—to have our back in any and every situation. Even in the midst of pain and suffering, we can access our own great well of love. When the body is not responding the way we desire, we can be intentional with ourselves.

What would happen if you were able to love yourself regardless of your back pain, migraine, or incontinence? In each and every situation, we have the opportunity to press in and love unconditionally—and to learn from the beauty of our own pain, which is begging for an opportunity *to speak.*

7

Be Satisfied

"Deep contentment is the visible sign of love.
Whenever a person is in love, he is in deep contentment.
Love cannot be seen, but contentment, the deep satisfaction
around him . . . his every breath, his every movement,
his very being—content."
– *Osho*

You are not a victim to the body you were born into. I know it's easy to blame your mom for having large thighs, or your dad for his excitement for heaping portions, but at some point, your body becomes your responsibility. It's important to recognize this to move into the space beyond it. Until you understand that *you create your reality; your choices have an impact*, we can't get to the good part—the part where we can begin discussing matters of satisfaction.

Because the diet industry demonizes certain foods and ways of eating, we crucify ourselves. Man, that's sexy—isn't it? We are force-fed images of thin, sweaty people, with the illusion that if we just start dieting, we too can look like an airbrushed model. Moreover, we are sold the lie that if we do not look a certain way, we do not deserve to feel sexy, to enjoy sex. We learn that our bodies are not deserving of celebration.

Our culture makes us judge our food and the plates of others. It robs us of nights out on the town when our jeans don't fit. It creates anxiety around social events because of fear of overeating. It deprives us of pleasure—from delicious cake to delicious sex. It facilitates the idea that pleasure should be earned. It makes us question if we are worthy to eat a slice of pizza. *Have we earned it?* It makes us fast all day before a hot night on the town with our favorite sweetie. *Will they be able to tell we've eaten lunch?* It's absurd. It has us questioning whether we are allowed to feel settled in our lives if we ate that sandwich and fries and *didn't* go to the gym.

We have been programmed to actively allow these violating opinions into our lives. At what point, do we question everything we've been taught? And if we have the power to question, we then can no longer be a victim to diet culture.

If we wake up, we have the potential to choose what we want to believe. We don't have to buy weight loss magazines or follow fitness social media accounts to feel good about ourselves. We know, on an intellectual level, that the model featured in the swimsuit ad is photoshopped and airbrushed, but deep down we are still judging ourselves and making ourselves *wrong* for not looking that way.

They are trying to sell a product at the cost of the consumer's self-esteem. When are we, as a society, going to take back our power and say *Enough is enough* to unrealistic beauty standards? When are women going to take back their bodies, their lust for life, and their pleasure?

There's something so addictive about observing the profile of someone who seems to have life all figured out. There's a mix of envy, anger, and desire. Do you know the feeling? I do.

Once, I was following this "perfect" mama with the "perfect" body and the "perfect" husband. She showed videos of her healthy breakfast in the morning, her child napping peacefully while she did her workouts, and her indulging with ice cream while displaying her six-pack.

Deep down, I knew these were the snapshots of only the idyllic moments, not the hard ones. Still, I desired her effortless flow to look, live, and feel great. I ached for the life she portrayed, never allowing myself to consider that—she probably did too! We often present our online lives as we wish they were—never as they are. Once I sat with this truth, I stopped following her and instantly got my sanity back. When I felt tempted to look, I instead chose to appreciate my relationships, my body, and the ebbs and flows of my life.

It is challenging to unfollow influencers who sell the "perfect" narrative. But it is the quickest way to remember our identity and restore our peace of mind. It isn't easy to stop obsessing over "Instagram porn," but it *really is* a simple formula: quit following accounts that make you feel bad about yourself! Take control of your narrative by teaching the algorithm what you *really* want to see! *This* is taking responsibility for giving ourselves the lives that we deserve.

In my journey to loving my body, I knew I was healing because I started appreciating the bodies of women around me. I could celebrate their beauty, uniqueness, and sexuality. This became a practice. I encourage people to consciously try to celebrate all bodies—tall, short, muscular, petite, voluptuous, and thin, at all different ages.

Once we can find beauty in everyone, we can retrain our brains to stop comparing; once we stop seeing the world through the filter of *Am I enough?* to *Wow! Everyone has beauty!* we can learn to relax in our own uniqueness. I stopped judging them out of fear of not being enough.

Who am I to say that a woman who feels completely comfortable with exposing her midriff shouldn't wear that crop top? I began to applaud women who were all shapes and sizes that seemed inspired by showcasing their bodies. They wore clothing that made them feel empowered and sexy. So, I took notes.

Slowly, positive messages began to eclipse negative ones.

There was no more:

Am I as thin as she is?

Are my arms bigger than hers?

I began to recognize my negative and shameful thoughts as they were brought to the light and was intentionally releasing them.

Diets don't work. It bears repeating—*diets don't work*. The diet industry profits when people fail. They prey off women who could be embracing their bodies and living a dynamic life, by making them believe there is something wrong with them.

In Christy Harrison's book, *Anti-Diet*, she presents us with intelligent data around dieting and how our body can go into survival mode if we push it too much. She goes into depth on why our bodies will do everything they can to maintain our weight. When we are actively trying to lose weight, our bodies kick into starvation mode. The brain triggers a response to hold on to any and all food that is coming in. In its endeavor to keep us from losing weight, our body finds ways to prompt us into eating more.[9]

Have you ever had the experience of doing really well on your diet? Your exercise routine is feeling strong. You are in a really good groove, and then one day, you struggle to wake up, and your head won't lift from the pillow to the sound of your alarm. Or maybe you're doing well, but you start compulsively craving oily and sugary food that you wouldn't ever crave even when you weren't dieting.

I have been there. I would beat myself up for *doing it wrong*. Little did I know, it wasn't *me* driving my decisions. It was my body trying to keep me safe.

This can feel like sabotage—but it's just biology. Sorry to report, we weren't built for starvation. It's inconvenient, I know. Our bodies want us to be healthy. And our idea of ideal weight and our bodies may be different. Often, our efforts for weight loss trigger a famine response. Willpower only goes so far, and then the body takes over. If we are in survival mode, our inner tyrant bites the dust. At that point, we are rendered powerless to our own defenses. We must learn to work with our body and not against it.

A recent study by a major behavioral weight loss program showed that the *average* participant lost around ten pounds in six months and kept *half of that* off for two years. We can become so obsessed with the

---

9   Harrison, Christy. *The Anti-Diet*. Little, Brown Spark, 2019.

promised relief of weight loss, we aren't reading the truth of this research:
Work really hard to lose weight, and two years later, half of your efforts
will be in vain. There is a reason the before and after pictures in these
program ads don't include pictures of the person years later.

I know it sounds insane to those who have been inundated with
diet culture, but it's really simple: Weight change isn't a simple "eat less,
exercise more" formula. As we learn the practice of self-care, we find
that the by-product is self-love.

How do you love yourself? We hear the message all the time, but
how does one *begin*? I'm all about practical application, so this book is to
serve as your resource for growth. I like to start with baby steps because
I know the simplest thing can also be the hardest thing.

So, for starters, how would you speak to your own best friend? Start
paying attention to your inner dialogue. When you're being critical, pull
back, and for no reason at all, I implore you—*Be kind to yourself* like you
would your bestie. Make that your new goal. This is the recipe for having
peace with your body and food. Simple, yes. Easy? Well, we'll get there.

It's a mental shift, and people typically desire instant gratification.
This won't be a quick resolution. If it were easy to have body acceptance,
there wouldn't be so many fitness plan books on the market. And there
wouldn't be so many people around, wasting their money on them,
hoping they work.

Paths are not linear. There are curves, dips, peaks, valleys, and
unexpected turns. This is an accurate portrayal of my recovery journey
with my body. As you read this, I am still healing and learning ways to
better love myself. It's a lifelong process.

I am not going to sugarcoat anything in this book and pretend that
if you follow my steps, your life will be automatically happy, and you
will never think about food again. That's just not how resolution comes.
It requires intentionality, introspection, listening, carving out time, and
trusting your intuition—a lot of things we cannot *see*. It's hard to build
discipline around the internal and blame the external for our issues.

Once we decide to change our lives, the divine brings opportunities for us to keep our promise to ourselves. This may come in the form of a challenge to strengthen our choice for change. It may look like a reprieve from our problems for the time being. It may even look like all hell has broken loose. *It has happened to all of us at one point or another.*

Kathleen had been on a great track with stopping her negative self-talk and comparing herself to others. She was finding more peace with her body, which was translating to more peace in her life. Then came the ultimate test: "I ran into an old friend from college that I always felt ugly around," she said. "As usual, she was looking so good with her perfect body and coiffed hair. My initial response was to internally tear the woman down: *Who does she think she is wearing those short shorts?* This quickly transitioned to, *I feel so frumpy.* I then just stopped and decided to connect with her from my heart. She ended up sharing about her life and her challenges with her disabled child. Immediately, I was struck with remorse and empathy and we bonded. In the end, I realized that if I would have stayed in my body negativity—I would have missed out on a beautiful opportunity to connect."

After we see ourselves as a warrior, we can take the next step in experiencing ownership over our bodies. That means learning to have more fun, to indulge, and to play.

There is a correlation to food, body shame, and pleasure. For whatever reason, most women just don't feel like they are allowed to have it. They don't know how to ask for it. They don't know how to care for themselves.

Do you need someone to give you permission to feel sexy in your own skin? I'll be that person. I am waving the magic wand of permission. Ask yourself, *In what areas do I feel I lack permission?*

Do I have permission to feel great in a bathing suit?

What if it's a bikini? Do I still have permission?

What if we're eating chips on the beach in said bikini, do I still have permission?

Where does this permission stop—and who decides?

Give yourself permission to experiment with self-acceptance in a new way. And come into full acceptance of the notion that *Perfect is boring.*

It truly is. The unique characteristics of our bodies are the magnificent peculiarities that make them worth celebrating.

My life began to change significantly once I realized that I needed help. Not just *read a fitness magazine with brightly colored pages and call it a day* kind of help, but real help. Luckily, I had the awareness in myself to understand, I *needed* support from others. We all do! We are a communal species.

As I dove deeply into my beautiful life, I actively fought the temptation to suffer over the size of my portions and arms. Odd, isn't it? We are *tempted* to suffer.

Until finally, with the help of a therapist, I joined Overeaters Anonymous: a 12-step program similar to Alcoholics Anonymous, but instead of alcohol, it combats issues with food and weight. While I no longer vibe with OA, it was exactly what I needed at that point in my life to save my booty!

Some people in the room struggled with anorexia, some with bingeing, some were emotional eaters like me. Lucky for me, these birds of a feather saved my ass. I finally had people who spoke my language, who understood what I was talking about, and could *laugh* about it—and cry about it—because no one understood why I could not be satisfied with my reality. There, I learned other people like me existed in the world, and I felt compelled not only to heal, but to be an example through my work after I recovered. In the program, I learned that I was coping through my obsession with food and weight when I did not have tools to turn over my grievances to my higher power.

Once I did, life began to shift dramatically. Then I stopped eating chocolate and dessert to punish myself. I started working on the deeper issues and stepped off the scale. I was overcome by a sense of relief because I didn't have to fight it anymore. I had permission to rid myself of the mental noise that chocolate endlessly created.

I recognized that my jumping-off point was fear. I was afraid that accepting my body meant that I would be doomed to gain weight, feel terrible about myself, and forfeit my favorite clothes. At that point, I still equated extra flesh to being unlovable. I also equated surrendering to being weak. After all, I believed in God, but I wasn't entirely trusting God was working on my behalf. My lack of belief was hindering my ability to be satisfied.

As sure as I know my mother is going to buy Aspen a birthday gift, in the way my child is sure I will pick him up from school and put him to bed each night—we must choose to be sure there is something greater working on our behalf—that God wants us to be healthy *and* happy. Furthermore, we must accept the fact that control never works in the long term.

Any time I tried to micromanage my food because I wanted to lose weight, it never benefitted me past a few weeks. Inevitably, I would become obsessed, and the head rush kept me from processing my emotions (which almost always, ironically, kept the weight *on*).

It wasn't until I started prayerfully approaching my issues that I truly realized it's about the internal. After I was able to recognize that I needed help sifting through my emotions and past experiences, energetic healing miraculously made its way into my life. *When the student was ready, the teacher appeared!*

Reiki found me.

For those who are not familiar with the practice: Reiki is a hands-on healing technique that balances and realigns energy while activating your own healing powers. It reduces stress, increases focus, restores vitality, and brings wholeness to your life.

The practice works by releasing stress in your body spiritually, physically, and emotionally—so that you can heal. It is an empowering spiritual modality. Because of it, I have witnessed many lives being transformed right in front of my eyes.

Reiki's biggest gift is its ability to expand our capacity to give and receive love. Victimhood and negativity melt away; in their place comes empowerment and love. Deeper wounds begin to heal, opening a person to a life that is fully their own with a greater capacity to manifest and accept all of life's gifts.

The best way to learn about Reiki is to dive right in. That's certainly what I did, not expecting what lesson it would have for me.

Synchronistically, I found Reiki at an OA meeting. During one session, I observed a woman sitting back with a slight smile on her face, eyes closed, with one hand on her heart and the other on her belly. I immediately felt annoyed by this woman. I couldn't believe the audacity she had to love herself openly in public!

In hindsight, I realize I was activated by the woman's *ease* because I felt deeply intrigued. After the session, I asked her what she was doing. She told me all about Reiki and took me to my first Reiki circle.

Seven centuries ago, the beloved Sufi scholar and poet Jalaluddin Rumi penned a line that still resonates with readers across the globe today. He is said to have written, "What you seek is seeking you." Because let's face it—getting healthy is not always conventional, and it is certainly not linear. What my body craved was divine connection and love, and that's exactly what Reiki had in store for me!

When I attended my first Reiki circle, I felt like I was coming home. With tingles throughout my entire body, I discovered a new peace and a sense of clarity that I had never felt before. Afterward, I decided Reiki and I were so compatible—I needed to become a Reiki practitioner. As I allowed myself to lean in, my relationship with my body began to heal. At first it didn't make sense. But soon, I learned to release my unreasonable expectations for myself and to *be satisfied* with my body. In turn, I was able to relinquish my internal judgements, a lifetime of toxic shame, and the external attachments that were holding me back from unconditional self-acceptance.

If I trust you—will I gain weight? I asked the voice.

Truthfully, that was not the case for me. I was kind to my body, and my body cared for me in return. In time, I was able to find the sweet spot between emotional eating and starving. I learned how to listen to my desires and give myself what I need. My first courageous step forward involved healing my relationship with chocolate—delicious, smooth, chocolate. I allowed myself the indulgence of dessert without fear, without antagonism—with full permission.

The more my inner bestie gave me the green light to eat whatever I wanted, the less I was tempted to binge. If I did eat several servings, I did so shamelessly, thereby letting go of the restrict-binge cycle. I was liberated to taste. To savor. To enjoy. I learned my limits; my sense of fullness, and how to honor myself by putting my fork down when I was satiated. And if I overindulged, that was okay too. Food no longer had to be *perfect* for me to feel worthy or to feel good about myself.

Over time, I began to feel healthier than ever—spiritually, mentally, and physically. I made peace with the things I couldn't control and allowed myself to relax into indulgence. In turn, I learned to *be satisfied*—with what my body needs, wants, and deserves. I boldly relinquished the shame that was blocking me from enjoying my life and experiencing every pleasurable sensation to the fullest.

8

Be Nourished

Dear Food,
   I wish it could have been easier for us. What do I say to something that has brought me everything from joy to sorrow in a matter of seconds? I have felt shame, guilt, pleasure, and excitement all in one breakfast. The pain when I couldn't stop consuming you makes me remember my frustration. I recall the excitement that would penetrate my body when I saw a plate full of cookies, followed by the self-disgust that would surge through my veins as I binge-ate every last one. There were times that I wished you never existed.

   I have heard it said that recovering from food issues is the most difficult because with alcohol and drugs, the remedy is abstinence. With food, the temptation comes out at least three times per day. This has made it difficult to enjoy you. I wish we could have found respect for each other. I know it's my fault.

   People say that you are neutral, and it is my reaction to you that matters. I understand but it isn't my fault that you tempt me with your yumminess. Maybe you needed to listen to me more. Why did God bring you into the world if only to bring pain to me?

   Still, I have decided to stop blaming you. I want to find peace when you are in the room and on my plate. I want to be able to appreciate you and also respect myself, and so, I lean into gratitude.

   Thank you for all that you have done for me. You have been my friend when I couldn't take care of myself. You were always there when I didn't know how to handle my life, or when I was stressed out. Thank you for your daily presence. Everywhere I looked, you were there, willing to soothe my pain and discomfort. I am sorry that I abused you and didn't enjoy you. I devoured you without savoring all the flavor and pleasure that you had to offer. You never seemed to mind. I was obsessed with you. I thought of you morning and night. Over time, this became destructive for me. I had to learn better ways to enjoy you.

As I worked on myself, I searched for any part of you that could make me feel safe. Prior to my decision to work on our relationship, restriction was the only way I felt secure in our connection. I didn't trust the pleasure of food. I didn't know recipes could be both nourishing and delicious. So, I'd limit myself: no fat, sugar, gluten, dairy, grains, nuts or meat. I felt the most grounded when I was eating—nothing.

Food, I know you exist to make me strong, and I have found peace around you; now, we can healthfully relate.

My happiness matters to me, which is why I want to be friends with you. Not just say-hello-to-you-at-the-grocery-store friends, but let's-vacation-together friends.

Thank you, food, for being patient with me.

Like any good relationship, I am now listening. I want to honor your purpose. When I don't allow your nourishment, I disrespect you. I will do my best to find other ways to fill my emotional needs somewhere else. Your contribution provides me with pleasure, nutrition, entertainment, health, and healing. I am still learning how to find balance with you in my life, but I have no hard feelings anymore toward you.

Can we be friends?

Love Your BFF,

Marla

xoxoxo

9

Be Sober

"Somewhere inside that hurting body, there is something
better, something stronger, something real."
– *R.M. Drake*

Few things boost serotonin like a fast-food bender when we're sad, sick, or stressed. A large fry to go is easily obtainable. It's legal. It's satisfying. It fills our stomach and takes the edge off when we are anxious. Stress bingeing can give us a sense of groundedness when we're out of control—weight in our bellies stills us when we are spinning out. The momentary chemical high it gives our brains is enough to keep us coming back for more: a stacked, double cheeseburger at midnight, please. *After all, I had a coupon!*

We are emotional, pleasurable, and sensual people. Food falls in alignment with all these things. We eat to be social while hanging out with friends and at parties. We eat to celebrate holidays and traditions. I am grateful for food for helping me deal with life's challenges.

Emotional eating can feel very shameful. We have no place to hide when we realize that we're hurting ourselves more than sustaining our bodies. For some, this is a lifelong or familiar battle. If you are reading this book, that is likely you. My hope is that this work is a tool that will help you find peace with the unhealthy eating patterns in your life, so that you can come to enjoy a relationship with food that is both nutritious and fulfilling.

Elizabeth came to me in misery around emotional eating: "Please, help me. I'm bingeing every time I get home from work. I can't stop eating potato chips. I've gained ten pounds, and still, I can't stop."

Elizabeth vowed to stop buying any junk food and keep only healthy food in her house.

She believed if she controlled her food, she would stop binge-eating and lose weight. The problem with her approach is that it only works temporarily. We must eat eventually, and the off-limit foods only make us crave them more. Deprivation kicks in along with high emotions, and once again, emotional eating takes over.

The solution is to consider *why* the emotional eating is happening.

I assured Elizabeth that by finding her *why*, she could stop the behavior. She noted that work was very stressful for her, that there was a specific colleague whose behavior constantly triggered her into shame and anxiety spirals. When we dug deeper, she spoke of a friend in seventh grade who continually harassed her about being the teacher's pet. This woman at work reminded her of this time in her life—a fellow female preoccupied with Elizabeth's relationship with those in power. She could see that her younger self was feeling afraid and dealt with it by eating.

Elizabeth became aware that potato chips were a childhood favorite food that she was craving. She didn't even like them anymore, but she defaulted to rifling through a bag every time she was overwhelmed.

Once we worked together to heal this inner child pain, her emotional eating stopped. She didn't need the pattern anymore because she had other tools. Yes, she lost weight as a result, but most importantly, Elizabeth learned that when she has that itchy feeling that makes her want to eat a dozen cookies, or a bag of chips, it is an alert. It's a signal for her to look at how she's feeling, as opposed to micromanaging her food intake. Many people don't mind emotional eating; they see no problem with it until they have gained weight. Weight gain or not, using food as a coping mechanism doesn't work long term.

Emotional eating is a red flag that invites us to go deeper. We don't overlook the warning and try to turn the red flag blue by controlling our food. It's best to interpret emotional eating as a consequence of the *real problem*.

Our body thrives at 98.6 degrees. If the thermometer reads 103 degrees, we don't blame the thermostat, we find ways to get ourselves back to health. Thank you, *thermometer*, for letting us know how sick we have become. Thank you, *midnight eating binge*, for revealing it's time to go inward.

When emotional eating happens, our inner children are usually screaming at the top of their lungs. I tend to the wounds of inner Marla who feels sad and lonely; who self-comforts by eating everything in sight.

Do you get angry at this little girl? Or do you patiently wait until she feels safe? Do you soothe her? Tell her she is right to feel scared and upset? *Yes!* You do whatever you can to make her feel safe.

It is the same when we shame ourselves for emotionally eating. There is an aspect of us that is acting out and feeling scared. We default to overeating to establish safety. What we don't realize is that *we* are the source of our security. Nothing outside ourselves can bring us peace. Emotional eating not only happens when life is stressful, but also when it is exciting. Excitement for those who have experienced trauma in childhood can be an anxiety-inducing experience due to its unpredictability.

Gregory was out for dinner with his family celebrating his new job. Excited and full of himself, he had a couple of glasses of wine and a big piece of tiramisu. I believe there's nothing wrong with indulging in wine and pie. But the next day when we talked, he was feeling angry at himself. Instead of being proud of himself for his new job, he was back to feeling bad about his appearance.

Sometimes the anxiety of a new start and celebration overlap. This can create a sense of mania in our brains that leads to us shoveling finger foods at social events. I like to encourage my clients to examine their states when eating. *Are they on autopilot?* If so, why?

I pointed out to Gregory that sometimes we binge because life can feel *too surreal, too new, too good* even. Fear of success is real, and it can manifest through bingeing. Gregory admitted that when he was excited, he would overindulge. He felt more comfortable in his natural state of contraction. So, when he made the career move, he processed the change with a second, and third helping.

Think about it, my friend. Has there been a moment when life was going well, but you were waiting for the other shoe to drop? Sometimes it's hard to receive and can reflect beliefs of inadequacy or an issue of low self-worth. Happiness can be vulnerable, and paradoxically, sometimes feeling nice and relaxed for a brief period can catalyze a stress spiral. *Why?*

When our baseline state is stress, our bodies crave its consistency. A moment of *other* can knock us over, even if that *other* is positive.

Take Tina, for example. Her wedding day was magical, surrounded by family and friends who were celebrating her new life. She couldn't have been happier. As a result, she spent the night binge-eating cake in the hotel room as opposed to making love to her new husband. She couldn't pinpoint it at the time, but our work together revealed she didn't feel worthy of receiving all the love and attention she was being given. Eating cake was the only thing that made her feel shielded from that which was *other*.

Coming to terms with what we deserve can sometimes be an emotional lesson. Reiki has taught me how to let my heart expand. It has encouraged me to release any personal blocks to experiencing more love. I notice that everyone says they want the best job, most satisfying relationship, more money, and radiant health, but when the goods arrive—they sabotage it somehow. Their body can't receive it because of beliefs of unworthiness, fear, or shame.

By letting ourselves sit in the vulnerability of the unknown, we can receive. This behavior can heal our emotional eating and other practices that are impinging on the love we are meant to experience.

I was still in the process of learning this on the days surrounding my wedding. Our trip had already been magical; I was internally celebrating as we cruised down the Hana Highway in Maui. I was marrying my beloved, having awesome sex, and exploring a beautiful island. Olaf and I were high on life when suddenly, a jarring thought crept in:

God, I hope we don't wreck and die—that would be awful.

My stomach sank while envisioning the possibility and acknowledging no one is above experiencing senseless tragedy. Then I put my hand on Olaf's and chose a sense of peace.

As I reclined, dangling my bare foot out the window on the passenger side, I declared that a state of peace and goodness would be my new normal. I committed to actively letting go of harrowing, stressful, and unproductive thoughts. I took a deep breath and placed my hand over my heart; I imagined it expanding, and allowed my whole body to receive the beauty of the moment. I am sure if I hadn't taken this time to deem myself worthy, I would have binged or overeaten that night after a spiral—catalyzed by one jarring thought.

Go deep, my friend. Unearth what is not serving you and replace it with something that does. Instead of worrying about food, look at what is truly going on.

What's happening emotionally? What is the component of you that is sidestepping your needs? Food will never meet the place inside you that craves love.

It can be challenging to go into the deep, shadowy places of ourselves. But I assure you that on the other side of this discomfort and pain lies more joy. When we've released the shame surrounding our food, there's more opportunity for joy in our lives.

Track your emotional eating patterns. *When do they show up and what emotions are you avoiding?* Remove the emotion; look at it objectively and understand there is a *reason* you're bingeing. This question is not to activate shame. It is designed to acknowledge where you can love yourself differently.

What I discovered about myself is when I overate, giving myself time to feel the pain was crucial. I'd take a small amount of time to feel angry at myself. But I didn't stop there. I became an emotional detective, searching for the root of *why* I was upset. Even if I thought it was frivolous, I didn't discount my feelings. For example, if my friend cancels plans with me because she is sick, I might understand, but it doesn't mean I am not upset about it. Those feelings have a place, especially because they may have a link that needs attention.

So, I'd give myself time to be with my feelings, cry in the shower, yell in the car. I'd let myself be over the top without hurting myself or someone else. It's better to get the feelings out rather than to eat over them.

Additionally, I became aware of the times when I emotionally ate. I would usually be triggered when visiting family over the holidays. I would do my best to accommodate everyone's needs and my own, which would result in my being tired, wired, and stressed. Food and drink are an easy numbing agent for complicated emotions.

After discovering this, I began to set myself up for success before going home. I would make a list of ways to support myself, so I didn't need to overeat. I put rules in place such as:

I don't show up to a gathering when I'm actively triggered by someone.

I ensure I'm hydrated and well-fed upon arriving.

I carve out meditation time every day on the trip to keep my sanity.

I've thought out my boundaries ahead of time and practiced articulating them.

Prevention and self-care made those visits with family more easeful.

The tricky part was when that familiar feeling of being on edge started to creep in. Sometimes, I'd act before thinking; the momentum was too strong to step away. If possible, I'd shift my attention, move my body, be around people I love, get out of my head and into my body—whatever tension reliever felt best, I'd do it.

Even if I did overeat, I'd applaud myself for being aware. Over time, I began to consider this as a game, and not *doom and gloom*. Every time a trigger occurred; I had a new opportunity to learn how to better care for myself.

Sometimes I succeeded and was able to stop the temptation to binge; other times—not so much, and guess what? That's okay. Because I'm human.

What separates non-emotional eaters from those who struggle with the pattern is that eating is not connected to their worth. They acknowledge they overate and move on.

In any case, slowing down to notice what is going on emotionally is vital.

It can be easier to numb out on food than deal with our emotions. Sometimes, we find there are deep-seated pains we need to address with a coach or therapist. I highly suggest this. We need someone else to hold space in these deep places where life feels wobbly. Being your own best friend means knowing when to find the right type of support for yourself. This isn't a solo journey. I don't know where I'd be without all my mentors, coaches, and therapists. In the words of the marvelous Barbra Streisand:

"People—people who need people are the luckiest people in the world." I can hear her belting that out as a reminder that while healing is not for the faint of heart, it is optimal to lead a nourished, fulfilling life.

Does this chapter resonate with you? Do you find yourself turning to food when you're feeling stressed, anxious, or upset? Then I urge you to take part in my free video mini-course, "Breaking the Cycle of Emotional Eating," which offers Seven Key Steps to Healing our Relationship with Food. You'll find it here: https://goloveyourbodyloveyourself.com/emotionaleating[10]

Our happiness is *worth* all the time and energy it takes to feel good.

---

10   Marla Mervis-Hartmann, "FREE Breaking the Cycle of Emotional Eating Mini-Course: Seven Steps to Finding Freedom with Food," https://goloveyourbody-loveyourself.com/emotionaleating.

10

Be Confident

"You learn who you are by unlearning
who they taught you to be."
– Nikki Rowe

Being bombarded with images and ads from the media on what we look like and how we're not good enough, can be overwhelming. It creates unnecessary noise in our heads about how we *should* be. Because these *shoulds* are usually based in something entirely unrealistic, they can instigate a binge without us even realizing we've been triggered.

We might see a photoshopped magazine cover, see the headline about the next fad diet on the front, then throw ourselves into a shame spiral. Without recognizing the signs that we are upset, we might immediately default to eating food that makes us feel crappy that will distract us from the proper care we deserve—ultimately caving to self-abandonment.

This influx of messaging doesn't stop at our weight. If it's not about our pants size, then it's skin, hair, and nails advertisements. In every way, the message rings loud and clear: *You are not enough!*

Advertisers and media know what they're doing. They know how to hit us in our weak spot. As a result, we become the vulnerable prey of marketing—desperate to fall for the hype. Money rules all when it comes to beauty standards; even more holistic brands demonstrate a parallel corruption. At the end of the day—Photoshop feeds families.

My favorite social post that I ever made was a photograph of me, "before" and "after." In the "after" picture, I made myself super skinny, then posted both pictures to Instagram. I was able to demonstrate the insanity of photoshop, and to my delight—almost everyone told me they liked my voluptuous picture better. It felt so good to poke fun at the insane measures we take to look nothing like ourselves.

Creating societal norms means the fashion and cosmetic industry can continue raising the bar. Millions of jobs depend on us feeling terrible about ourselves. They write the narrative, then remind us of our story every time we step outside the house. Imagine what it would cost them for us to be kind to ourselves, to stop carrying our bodies like an apology.

I see this all the time in my clients. Julianne came to see me and announced as she entered my office in a remorseful tone, "Oh, look at my butt in these jeans. I have no idea what I was thinking when I wore them today!"

Julianne, like many others, communicate their perceived inadequacies as though they are paying a toll to exist exactly as they are; as if to say, *Don't worry, I know I am not perfect, and if we both acknowledge that my butt is too big, then we're all good.*

God forbid we love our butts, and yes, I'm even talking about the cellulite. I can feel you cringing, because you've been conditioned to hate it, but imagine who you'd be if you didn't.

If women could embrace the shape of their nose, their crooked teeth, the size of their breasts, and the unique attributes that make their bodies absolutely gorgeous, they would be unstoppable. But unfortunately, centuries of wiring have taught women—*almost everything* can be wrong with our appearance. And, lucky us—the beauty industry has the solution!

I recognize even calling my business, *Love your Body Love Yourself* is triggering for some. But that's okay, because I like to get straight to the point. Call it consistent branding, but I like my clients to know what they are getting into when they schedule a session with me. I have one rule, and it's in bold print on my business cards, because I want to change the norm; I want my clients to want to change the norm.

In turn, I am quick to prescribe a *body appreciation* exercise to newcomers. It is as follows:

Relax. Create a space and carve out a small amount of time to get quiet with yourself and just *be.*

Breathe. Assume a meditative posture, and inhale deep into the belly, then exhale, repeat this several times until your nervous system is calm.

Appreciate. Begin silently or verbally speaking gratitude over the parts of your body that *work* for you—*and maybe even show some love to the ones that you don't favor.*

Show gratitude. Choose any body part that is currently causing you physical or emotional pain. Put your hand on it and feel the energy of gratitude penetrate your body.

Listen. As your hands are on each body part, tune into how you feel, and how it feels; speaking sweetly, ask it why it hurts.

Love. Speak love and healing over each part of your body that is tense, depleted or sore. Revel in appreciation over what that specific part serves and what it has taught you.

Get quiet. Ask your body what it's teaching you. Does it have any feedback about how you can be a better friend?

Apologize. Tell your body you are sorry for abandoning it.

Forgive yourself. I really can't emphasize this one enough.

Show appreciation for your practice. Hover your hands over your whole body, then bring yourself back into your surroundings with touch. Celebrate the fact that you took time to care for yourself.

Some other practical tools I give my clients include:

Affirmation baths. Get in the mirror and affirm yourself like crazy! No negative comments allowed; praises only.

Return to your body. When I start my work, I tend to get tunnel vision. I know, in between sessions, my body needs to move. It's important that I reconnect with myself. So, I shake. I dance. I stretch. It doesn't have to be for long periods of time. 2-5 minutes at most. This was a game changer for getting grounded. Food is no longer the only choice.

Work in time chunks. There's so much going on in the world, and there are so many pressures. That means we have to spend our time wisely and carve out hours for rest and reprieve. I find it challenging to do so when I am on a roll. But time and time again when I create boundaries around time, my body trusts me that I will take care of her. My body isn't the lowest priority on the totem pole.

My client Felicia decided to delete all her social media accounts. Not just delete them off her phone, but do away with them—forever. It was a big step for her that took a lot of courage. These days social media touches every aspect of life from panning events, finding our soulmate, or looking for work.

Felicia had grown up on Instagram since she was twelve and was uncertain of how life would feel without being plugged in. Every time she scrolled through her feed, she was left with feelings of inadequacy and failure.

"I know the images aren't real," she'd say, "but they still make me feel *less than*. It is depressing that all these women are spending tons of time and energy to give the illusion of perfection."

Felicia had had enough. She reported that she was compulsively eating as comfort, until it became a rebellion against social media. She felt depressed and her therapist suggested medicine. As Felicia was a powerful, strong, woman who loved to dive deep—she had a hunch she needed a different prescription. As someone committed to growth, she heard me out when I suggested social media was knocking her off center. Because she knew her own worth and could reclaim it at any time, she felt relief as she took her own power back and went off the grid.

As women, we buy into the belief that if we are not famous or successful in an area of our life, we are not doing something right. We can't all be Wonder Woman, and the steps it would take to get there would be crazy making. The strife to be perfect is all self-imposed.

These programmed notions of how we should *be* creating a type of suffering that can only stay under the surface for so long. Moreover, that suffering bleeds into our personal relationships and determines the way we do friendship and romance.

During my healing process, I began to realize I was never actually *present* in social situations. I was usually eyeing the snack table, weighing out whether I should indulge as my anxiety skyrocketed. There is an inevitable self-centeredness that comes with having to constantly curate our packaging. We become so consumed with how we look in our clothes, we miss out on celebrating life with our loved ones in real time.

We also derail our goals. Sometimes, learning to love ourselves takes precedence over our studies, our work commitments, and our family time. What kind of mom am I if I am always half removed from ice cream truck dates with my son? What kind of wife am I if I'm agonizing over the size of my belly while making love with my husband? These fears steal from our most valuable moments. And working through them made me seriously evaluate how I wanted to be a partner and mother—namely, that I did not want to always be half present and half satisfied constantly.

It became my goal to *raise my vibration* to change my life. By focusing on the positives about myself, I knew I'd be sending an outpouring of positive energy that had no choice but to return to me. I knew feelings of worthiness began and ended with me. So, I started outpouring acceptance all over myself. Worthiness never comes at a certain weight. If there's anything I've learned, it's that there will *always* be a lower weight to aim for and a higher bar to achieve.

Women who embrace themselves are magnetic. They understand they are allowed to let themselves shine. We can shine at any weight, especially if we are oozing love from our inner being. If we let ourselves feel beautiful all the time, acknowledging that our beauty isn't only about our looks, we will recognize that feeling desirable has nothing to do with our weight, wrinkles, or stretch marks. Our self-acceptance *is* the spark.

A wise colleague of mine, Debbie Lichter of Freedom Embodied Academy offered, *We must stop bonding over bitching*. If our friends start critiquing their bodies, we do not have to engage in the conversation. By entertaining ourselves with negative body talk, we infuse the space with detrimental energy. This can be uncomfortable at first, but put your big girl panties on and hold your boundary. This can help turn the conversation around. So, if your friends start talking about their latest diet, how silly they feel for wearing a bikini with their big gut, or commenting on someone else's weight gain or loss, it's perfectly reasonable to say—*Nothing!*

Yep, that's right, pull back, change the subject, or lovingly call them out on their negativity.

Really? *Are you really putting yourself down like that?* I wish you could see what I see. *A beautiful being that has more important things to do than focus on making yourself wrong. How about saying something nice about yourself? Right now!*

By eliminating the negative talk, we encourage other women to no longer participate in the culture they are creating. We must be committed to not passing negative body speech down to our children. If we want real leverage over toxic messages in the media, we must train our kids to speak kindly of themselves.

I teach Aspen to regularly focus on his qualities. Boys are just as much a part of the revolution our culture needs. My son is taught body positivity for himself, and for everyone. We change the eyes of the future generation by changing how we talk about our own bodies.

When Mae came to see me for the first time, she articulated something that I think most women struggle with: projection. Specifically, the way women project onto other women.

Mae had struggled with her weight and disordered eating throughout most of her life. She recalled an interaction with her close friend, Katie, who was close to six feet tall and rail thin, Mae seethed. She said Katie's most recent *upset* was about the 10 pounds she'd put on during her extended vacation. After the conversation, Mae became irritated, and internally spiraled into a binge—running from her own shame, frustration, envy, and self-loathing.

"It's frustrating because Katie will never understand what it feels like to *actually* struggle with her weight," Mae said angrily. While I held space for Mae's pain, I encouraged her to understand it was unfair to project that belief upon Katie, as Katie is entitled to her own reality, and Mae deserves to understand *it's not about her* and to love herself intentionally through these conversations.

Throughout our sessions, Mae understood that her pain was coloring her friends' experiences, and that with a little more attention inward, she could handle her feelings better in the moment. Mae also learned that her own appearance has nothing to do with Katie's, and it's best if we don't antagonize ourselves with comparison over something as beautiful and organic as the human body.

I've learned women, unfortunately, are often in quiet competition with each other. If one gal at the office is trying intermittent dieting—suddenly, everyone is on a fast. If one girl dives into the chips on vacation—suddenly everyone follows suit. It's an interesting notion that Mae presented in my office that day: Women betray other women as they betray themselves. It's important to recognize these patterns because it not only affects our friend groups, but it also affects the next generation.

Lack of confidence can be addressed by noticing our thoughts and feelings and challenging them. After we master our minds, we can get out of the way of our own success and thrive in body confidence. When we are bombarded by a thought that makes us wince, it's important for us to really consider, *Is it true?*

A very well-known quote and one of my favorites from Marianne Williamson applies here:

"Our deepest fear is not that we are inadequate. Our deepest fear is that we are powerful beyond measure. It is our light, not our darkness that most frightens us. We ask ourselves, 'Who am I to be brilliant, gorgeous, talented, fabulous?' Actually, who are you not to be? You are a child of God. Your playing small does not serve the world. There is nothing enlightened about shrinking so that other people won't feel insecure around you. We are all meant to shine, as children do. We were born to make manifest the glory of God that is within us. It's not just in some of us; it's in everyone. And as we let our own light shine, we unconsciously give other people permission to do the same. As we are liberated from our own fear, our presence automatically liberates others."[11]

It's our responsibility to be an example to others after we know the truth. That is what I have founded my practice upon—I strongly feel it is my calling. But I acknowledge how even the weight of *that* can be challenging. We must consider these things carefully and forfeit the urge to dim our light or diminish our beauty. Confidence can be especially scary if we feel we are the only ones stepping out. Or worse, if leaning into courage appears to cause pain to those around us. This was an especially hard lesson for me, as two difficult memories from childhood made me nervous about my own desire to thrive.

When I was in seventh grade, I was incredibly outgoing. I applied myself and was impassioned for theater and any opportunity to perform. When I would receive awards, my best friend was always there to support me. Because her parents were close to my parents, her mother and father would often be there to cheer me on. This was all wonderful until her dad began comparing her to me constantly.

"Why can't you just prioritize your studies, like Marla?" he'd say.

I could see my sweet friend's self-esteem flickering out. Though she never took her pain out on me, I know she internalized her father's comments, and they deeply affected us both.

A second memory that is equally as painful took place during my middle-school years. Once, I was at my friend's house looking for a piece of paper. On the desk, I discovered a notebook and found pages of notes between three of my closest friends. They were all about me: making fun of me with pictures and negative comments knocking down my gifts, my appearance, and my wardrobe. I was crushed. It was like the wind had been knocked out of me—by my best friends.

When I think about that moment, I can still feel a sting of enduring

---

11   Williamson, Marianne. *A Return to Love: Reflections on the Principles of a Course in Miracles.* Thorsons Classics, 2015.

pain. After that, I struggled to find safety to be myself. If I wasn't accepted among my best friends, where was I safe?

My mom lovingly cared for me by listening and giving me full permission to cry it out. My heart leaped when she said, "Wanna go for ice cream?"

Ice cream *always* helped.

It stilled every ache and celebration in my childhood. It was the key to my emotional regulation.

Boyfriend trouble? Ice cream. Lost volleyball game? Ice cream. Bad grade on a test? Ice cream. This period created my attachment to Rocky Road as a coping mechanism. My mom was soft, full of love, and had the best intentions.

I often wonder what would have happened if I would have fully processed these emotions in the moment, instead of grieving with indulgences.

Had my mom known taking me out on the porch to rock me would have been the better option, she would have done it. Had she known my coping skills would have been fueled by disordered eating, she would have protected me.

As parents, how can we know? We intuit the needs of our children and give them appropriate care in the moment. My mom did her best with the tools she had. She saw that ice cream calmed me and brought me comfort. Who wouldn't want that for their child? She didn't know that pushing down emotions with sweet treats is a slippery slope. She didn't understand the pain would surface with or without the food.

As a general rule, mother's hearts are in the right place. As a mother, I have a compassion for myself and other mamas in this situation.

What would I do for Aspen if he was upset? Give him ice-cream? Yes, maybe.

It is through this compassion that I can access empathy for all the parents hoping to raise a child with body acceptance and peace with food.

While those early memories can be chalked up to childish viciousness, they very much crafted who I am. We all have shaping moments that predispose us to shame spirals, dysfunctional coping mechanisms, and addiction. With love and support from our inner best friend, we can unpack these experiences and rethink the negative messages we adopted from them. Over time, we can establish a rock-solid confidence that makes us impenetrable to outside influences.

No doubt, it won't be easy; healing is challenging, but it will be worth it in the end. While most of us have never been taught how to handle our pain with the relentless compassion we deserve, coping without buckets of Ben and Jerry's in hand is possible.

Though this practice takes effort, patience, and courage, we must remember we are making our mark on our destiny. When we heal from our past stories, we have been told, we demonstrate power to other people and to our children. This teaches the next generation to courageously step into their strengths, leaving body shame in the dust.

11

Be Pain Free

"Take your pleasure seriously."
– Charles Eames

In the 1980s, Jane Fonda adopted the slogan, "No pain, no gain," for her exercise videos. This inevitably promoted the strife mentality of the diet industry. Since then, we have been influenced to believe if we want to look our best, we must endure blood, sweat, and tears. We also must be willing to compromise inordinate amounts of time *working on ourselves*, often in a state of deprivation.

Most of us have adopted Fonda's *no pain, no gain* mentality. This motto tells us we have to struggle, overwork, and push ourselves over the edge to get the body, career, money, and life that we want. This is certainly a Westernism, and a counterproductive way of relating to the human body.

The American Dream was built on the *no pain, no gain* mentality. To easily achieve our dreams is hardly applauded and often shunned. We become internal work horses.

Work hard.
Do more.
Stay Later.
Be stressed.

Workout longer.

Many of us feel that we don't deserve to enjoy our body unless we are beating up on ourselves, hitting the gym harder, white-knuckling our food, and micromanaging our meal plan.

In my experience, this painful existence was not sustainable. Throughout my twenties and thirties, it was the fastest route to illness and burnout. It gave me the opposite effect that I was searching for. Instead of achieving my body goals, this ruthless mentality would set me up for a binge.

My pep talks influenced by this concept sounded like this:

"Okay, Marla, this time we are gonna do it. No carbs, sugar, or meat. No food after 5:00 p.m. We can do it this time. We'll chew gum to cut cravings, and exercise a minimum of two hours per day."

Sounds extreme, huh? Yes. I am still recovering my adrenal glands.

It was a never-ending cycle of restriction and dieting coupled with overexercising. My willpower fueled my regime for at most a week, and then the compulsive eating would start. I'd consume all the food that I'd restricted in a week within a day.

To top it off, my overexercising left me exhausted and nursing an injury. My negative self-talk made me feel like a failure. My lack of self-care would make me feel unloved. It was a no-win for me. I could be miserable and starving, or miserable and binging.

I blamed myself for not working hard enough and ultimately failing. I felt like a loser for never being able to keep the pace up. Little did I understand that pain wasn't the answer. In fact, it was exacerbating all my issues.

Today, I thank God that it failed miserably. This wasn't the way we were destined to live. One of my teachers, Yogi Bhajan says, "Happiness is your birthright. Live it!"

We were born to be happy. It's a hard concept to adopt, I know. But what good friend wouldn't want her bestie to be blissfully happy? If we're going to hold ourselves accountable, let's do it in a way that truly benefits us. Let's check in with ourselves regularly.

Are we happy?

I'll tell you what makes me less than happy. Going to bed hungry. That doesn't bring me anything but agitation, insomnia, and the night munchies. Additionally, pushing my muscles to the point of fatigue until I'm in physical pain isn't love. Hitting the gym every day sounds great in theory, but giving our bodies no day of rest isn't happiness either.

I tell my clients—*pleasure is the strategy.*

Truly. It is the key to having a great relationship with our bodies and with food. And no. I don't mean instant gratification. There is no one-stop shop for this. Healing comes from the deep well inside of ourselves. It requires listening to our bodies to ensure we are on the right track.

Pleasure dismantles the *no pain, no gain* model by lavishing ourselves with good food, exercise that floods us with joy, and adequate rest. When we operate from a place of being *pleased* with ourselves, our angry, stressed out, inner tyrant is less emotionally hungry. As a result, we don't have false pangs of physical hunger induced by stress. So, we don't binge, restrict, or diet.

Pleasure is the guiding light that points us back to our intuition. Our intuition is our inner best friend's voice that will always guide us to what is best for us in the long term. Pain pulls us away from our intuitive, connected power source. When we let it rule our lives, it knocks us off-center and sabotages our efforts to thrive.

It's crushing to me when I see mothers in postpartum adopting the "no pain, no gain" mentality. They are all striving to "get their bodies back," when . . . their bodies have only done hard work to keep their children alive.

Heather came to me after her second pregnancy. She was committed to returning to her pre-pregnancy weight. "My body bounced back so quickly after my first pregnancy, but this second one is so much harder!" she exclaimed.

In between nursing and errands, she was doing YouTube videos for her abs and intense exercises. This misaligned action wasn't coming from pleasure. It was coming from the conditioned notion that our bodies are controllable and that we should be perfect.

As a certified "Elemental Body" postpartum practitioner for pelvis and abdominal issues, I can confidently tell you, that not only do sit-ups not work they will harm a woman who has just given birth. To make matters worse, Heather was already suffering from Diastasis Recti—the split in the "six pack" muscles that sits below your midline. If you suffer with this condition you know that it creates back pain, pelvic floor dysfunction, painful sex, incontinence, and the much dreaded "belly pooch."

The belly pooch is the demise of many women's self-esteem.

During postpartum, the body needs time to heal. It is the perfect time to go slow and friend yourself.

The body is designed to be soft and—in some cases—never bounce fully back. And that's okay. You are a changed being. You are now a mother.

I recognize there is great pain in that. I know—I am a mother too. As the body shifts sizes, it is a constant reminder that nothing is the same. Life is different. And there's not a lot of space for mothers to be in grief.

There's a cultural belief that we are *only* supposed to thrilled about this new baby. And yes, there is the sweetness and joy of giving birth. But that doesn't negate the depression and transition that many women face.

I encouraged Heather to consciously grieve. To grieve the body that she once had, to find peace with her body right now.

"Stop fighting yourself. It isn't working anyway. Your body is exhausted and in pain and you aren't present with your children!"

I supported Heather to let herself mourn—mourn the loss of her body, her identity, her lifestyle.

After some good crying, Heather was ready to listen to her body. She slowed down, and at times, this was uncomfortable. She moved through the discomfort and finally relaxed into a slow mode. This practice involved letting her belly heal with gentle exercises that I prescribed to her.

After a while, Heather began to find pleasure in her time of postpartum. After all, it is fleeting. She wanted to be compassionate to herself so that she could show up for this special time with her baby.

"Marla, there are moments when I long for my pre-mama body, but I know that those longings are hurting me and not in any way effective. I have decided to accept myself . . . and maybe—to one day even love my belly."

12

Be Attuned

"When many voices are speaking at once, listen to the one most quiet and gentle. That's the one worth listening to."
– *Miranda Linda Weisz*

Listening to the small voice inside us, that has our best interest at heart, is pivotal in the act of BE-Friending ourselves. You know that voice—the one that gives you deep premonitions about how a work situation will turn out? The one that says the person you are dating is not right for you, even though they are adorably cute?

In my Reiki classes, I teach my students how to become more connected to their intuition. "What if it tells me something I don't want to hear?" Dina asks apprehensively.

"Sometimes, that is the case," I tell her.

Inevitably, someone raises their hand, and notes that they can't access their intuition. Most likely because it has been dimmed for so long that they can't hear it. Let's be honest, sometimes listening to that voice is *scary*, especially when it comes to our body.

The bodily sensations of our inner knowing that we are hungry, paired with the inundation of messages we receive from society about how we should be *eating like a lady*, can create a sense of overwhelm. As a result, we surrender our power without recognizing it. This leaves us searching for wisdom outside of ourselves, when our intuition holds the key to our higher wisdom and almighty truth.

Kim Chestney, international best seller of *Radical Intuition* says, "Your intuition is the best friend you will ever have. Its mission is one thing, and one thing only: to lead you to your best life and authentic self. Once you learn to recognize the difference between your inner wisdom and outer conditioned thoughts and feelings, you will create an unshakable bond with your higher self, one that will guide you effortlessly through the decisions, challenges and growth opportunities of your life."[12]

This leads us away from searching Instagram for the newest fitness regimes or no-carb recipes to deal with our emotions. It leads us back to see what our inner guidance is saying: the quiet call that is always waiting for us to tune in.

When we don't know how to tap into our body's cues, the world around us becomes challenging to navigate. We can become confused about where we stand on a myriad of issues. This disconnection with ourselves can leave us feeling lost about what actions to take, and where our boundaries lie. Inevitably, we don't get the results we want in our lives and relationships. This creates deep shame which further catapults us out of listening to our inner truth and pushes us into trying to manipulate our lives with empty actions.

We lean into our *shoulds* and *to-dos*; we become reactive and push ourselves by dieting, restricting, overexercising, bingeing, and purging. This is when we become the most susceptible to social media's unending reel of *before and after* pictures, wondering if dramatic weight loss could be the remedy to all our pain. We wonder if we can shut up our inner discomfort by turning up the noise of the external.

Thin is vital to be accepted.

Our body is not thin, pretty, nor curvy enough.

Stop eating grains, legumes, and fruits.

Have you tried the ice cream diet?

12   Chestney, Kim. *Radical Intuition: A Revolutionary Guide to Using Your Inner Power.* Novato, CA: New World Library, 2020.

The hamster wheel begins. We are brainwashed. Even worse, we rarely stop to question it.

These voices are not exclusive to the media. They can belong to our family and friends. The opinions of those closest to us can especially wreak emotional havoc on us, and create internal misunderstandings, even with ourselves. After this internal turmoil starts, we spiral into panic and overindulge. The emotional eating cycle begins.

We reach the bottom of the chip bag and wonder how we got so offtrack. When in reality, we were never on the right path—our own path—to begin with.

We cannot be-friend a body we are not properly in tune with. We cannot separate the human body from the spirit. If those two things are not in alignment, we will listen to outside cues about our own well-being and find ourselves more lost than ever.

Tara was afraid to go hang out with her friends because they always drank alcohol and ate food that didn't work for her. Guaranteed, if she joined, she felt the social pressure of others pushing her to join in. She loved her friends but didn't know how to navigate these awkward social situations.

This issue of boundaries is one we are all acquainted with. Holidays, parties, and family gatherings are the true test of our mental fortitude. These events emphasize the importance of knowing our own truth. Too easily, it can be derailed by the desire to belong, which is ingrained in all of us. According to Maslow's hierarchy of needs, a feeling of belonging is essential to a healthy existence. As the poet Maya Angelou eloquently says, "I long, as does every human being, to be at home wherever I find myself."

Taking actions that are against the grain of our tribe can bring up feelings of vulnerability and fear. That vulnerability can look like prideful rebellion or submission to the crowd. This is a normal response. Doing the brave, aligned thing is sometimes the hardest course of action, even if it's small.

How would your best friend show compassion to you to help you ease your mind? Would they encourage you to listen to yourself or force you to go with the crowd?

During my more than ten years of recovery, I would experience stretches of grace with my body. At the beginning, those stretches might have been one week. But the longer I healed, the longer they lasted. Still, every now and then my sense of safety with food would be interrupted by obsession rearing its ugly head, interrupting my meditation, and I couldn't seem to get answers as to why I was doing all the work and *still* suffering.

Simply put, it was because I was afraid to listen to my truth and was still micromanaging my food and weight. At first, it was unbearable to become present with my body. But I chose to connect with myself. As I got quiet, took a breath, and listened—thoughtful questions began to surface:

If I were to listen to my body and connect to my intuition, what would happen?

If I were to listen and follow body cues with food, what would happen?

If I were to listen to how my body wanted to exercise, what would happen?

What is the fear that is keeping me from BE-Friending myself?

Through carefully considering these things, I discovered a younger Marla inside of me that was scared and alone. She was petrified to accept her body. This younger Marla thought attention and love were conditional on her appearance, that without a restricted regimen, she couldn't be loved. This misunderstanding needed to be resolved.

So, I went inside and loved the petrified part of me. I found my own inner mother and comforted my scared, inner little girl.

Little Marla? my Inner Mother asked, *why do you feel you need to strive to be loved?*

Little Marla responded, *If I do not do everything perfectly and look good while doing it, no one is ever going to choose me . . . and I will be alone.*

This pained me to hear. Still, I just listened. I didn't make Little

Marla wrong, no matter what she had to say. I reminded her that it was safe for me to listen to my body and to eat how my body wants. Slowly over time, the fear subsided. One meal at a time, I nurtured myself in a way that made sense to me. Every time I was afraid I didn't look *good enough*, I reminded the younger Marla that she is loved unconditionally.

Through the willingness to listen to my fear, I found my core belief: *If I gain weight, I will not be loved.*

Identifying our core beliefs and working with them is the key to making massive shifts in the relationship between our bodies and food. If we don't address the fear, the unconscious part of ourselves that wants to keep us safe can often take us offtrack.

FOMO: the fear your partner may not be attracted to you, or fear of a family member judging you can instigate a shame spiral. When we name our fears, we can create safety for ourselves. Without knowing our fears, we flail around in the dark looking for answers that won't work.

By allowing ourselves to feel the fear and address the underlying misunderstanding, we spotlight and dissolve shame with self-compassion. This gives room for a new behavior to manifest. Self-love heals. Time and time again.

I understand the discomfort, my friend. It's true. You may uncover something that isn't easy to handle on your own. Or you may not be able to access this fear without the support of someone else. *That's okay.* We all need each other. Find someone who can help you—a coach or therapist that is trained in this work who can champion you in the way you deserve.

I would have never made it to my happy place with my body if it weren't for my support system who has taught me how to be-friend myself—my loving Guides, who affirm the messages we are already intuiting are invaluable. Build community with those who are intentional about listening to their own *True North*, who can point you inward in moments of weakness, to your own pillars of resilience and truth.

13

Be Angry

"When angry, count four. When very angry, swear."
– *Mark Twain*

My fingernails were my weapon of choice as a child. They were something silent I could sink into my sisters' skin when I'd had enough. I have to say, *I am sorry, Sissies!* I truly didn't know a better way to communicate myself.

"Marla never makes waves. She is such an easy child," my mom would say.

That's me. Middle child. Libra. Keeper of the peace. I hate disharmony or anyone being upset. I will twist myself into a pretzel to ensure everything runs smoothly.

Growing up, I would *go with the flow* in conflict until I couldn't handle it anymore. Once I'd hit my limit, I'd wait until my mom wasn't looking and dig my fingernails deep into the arms of whichever sister was infuriating me in the moment. Inevitably, they'd let out a bloodcurdling scream. *Rightfully so.* Then my mom would respond with shock that her peacekeeping daughter could be so rageful. Her shock would accelerate my shame about acting out, and I would quickly remember the love and attention that I got from being easygoing. Then I'd resort to keeping my anger at bay once more.

It wasn't until my adult years that I felt like I could appropriately access my anger. It was buried below the surface, melded with sadness and fear. In my younger years, I felt scared of it in my body. So, I would repress it to keep it from robbing me of the validation of being *a good girl*.

By default, I robbed myself of having a regular outlet for the anger that seemed to be compounding as the years passed. I was more comfortable with turning my anger inward than dealing with a loved one who continuously, unknowingly or knowingly, violated my boundaries.

As an adult, I would feel the electricity in my fingers pulsate when I'd get upset. Instead of digging them into anyone's skin—*because hey, that's crazy, right?* I acted out by shoveling food into my mouth instead. The third or fourth cookie always helped me push those feelings down.

I can't tell you the amount of chocolate I have eaten compulsively because of my discomfort in feeling angry. I used food to cope with any emotion that didn't feel right.

I was living in a constant state of discontent with low-grade anger building in my body. The issue with anger is that it can too easily become the norm. It's the silent killer; after it's packed away in our bodies, it's there to stay.

My favorite remedy for anger was food. I used it to stuff frustration down, and it eventually ended up in my bladder. It took me years of experiencing bladder infections and symptoms of interstitial cystitis to learn how to address my emotions in a healthy way that didn't leave me on antibiotics, rolled in a ball, with a hot-water bottle on my pelvis.

With any physical ailment, I have always addressed it physically and emotionally. As a Reiki master, I learned early on that we store our emotions into our body. As I began to study the chakra system—the energy center in the body—I found that the bladder will hold onto anger and fear. Louise Hay, an early pioneer of energy medicine, referred to the angry bladder as being *pissed off.* [13]

As I began to take responsibility for my bladder pain, I became

---

13   Hay, Louise L. *You Can Heal Your Life*. Sydney: Hay House, Inc., 2017.

empowered to heal myself. Learning foods that aggravated me, doctor care, herbs, and lots of Reiki were helpful. However, the true remedy was letting go of the victim mentality of physical pain and getting intimate with the emotions that lived in my bladder—*anger.*

Though any form of upset is not *who we are*, these emotions can show up in the way we present ourselves in the world, sometimes to our detriment. Emotions are meant to flow through us. We are not our stress or feelings, but if we don't express them, they become us, showing up in our personality. Maybe you are snippy with your family over nothing, maybe you get depressed easily, or maybe your discontent is impossible to hide, and flashes of feeling always show up in your face. As a result, our relationships are impacted by our unprocessed emotions.

Many of my clients have shared with me how scary it is to experience their anger. They would prefer to bottle it up than to learn how to manage it properly without harming themselves or others. Many women don't realize that their unwanted eating, specifically bingeing and purging, comes from unexpressed feelings.

Samantha's mother taught her early on that money wasn't to be trusted. The family had been wealthy for years, then had to sell everything to move in with her grandparents. This pattern was repeated many times in her childhood. She felt deep disgust and anger toward her parents for creating this unsettled upbringing. She was sure that their frivolous spending could have been avoided. Her unprocessed anger left her in the toxic cycle of starving and bingeing. Her experience with money mirrored her relationship with food.

When Samantha finally decided to take her power back, her body healed, and her food issues subsided. Of course, this didn't happen overnight. I am certainly not making claims for a quick recovery. It took time to learn how to deal with anger and readjust her coping mechanisms.

Samantha's story encouraged me to slow down and become intimate with my own anger. Giving it the spotlight helped me make significant shifts. It can feel excruciating to *feel* frustration and anger and not simply leave our bodies, or shove it down so we do not feel.

But guess what? I have done it. I have lived to tell the story. And my discomfort did not kill me. Sitting with my frustrations has made me stronger and more attuned with what I need to process in my life.

I grabbed my journal and began to purge my fears and anger. My worries and rage about my body were readily accessible: the sadness that I didn't look the way I wanted, the resentment at food and how it'd betrayed me—it all poured out. Before long, the floodgates were open, and I began to process a myriad of *other* unexpected emotions. As a result, an exercise for my practice was born.

This was my template:

If I allow myself to be angry, sad, resentful about_____, I would admit_____.

Depending on the topic, I let myself take up as many pages as I needed. After several sessions of journaling, I realized beneath my body issues were the roots of all my untouched resentments toward other things. The ones I could never hear, because I was too busy drowning my pain with food and external noise.

I wrote about anything or anyone that made me feel anger. I spewed it all onto paper. I got it out of my body daily and whenever I felt those lurking feelings. The earlier I was aware of my beliefs, the easier it was for me to sit down and process. I learned I didn't have to be afraid of myself. My feelings were my friend the entire time.

After I built a relationship with writing, relief began to surge through my body as I crumpled up the most recent list of resentments and threw them away. I felt years of unprocessed emotions release. I expressed the upset, then let go.

We do not realize that faulty beliefs can add physical weight to our bodies. The body is just a manifestation of the soul. If we are carrying around beliefs such as:

I don't have time to take care of myself.

I'll never find a partner.
I'll never be as good as_____.
I don't deserve_____.
My dreams never come true.

They *will* manifest physically. Examining these beliefs can help us go deeper with ourselves and unearth blockages in many areas of our lives. As a result, we can divorce beliefs from emotions and emotions from food. By getting to the true culprit of our unhappiness, we can break free from negative body image and food behaviors that don't serve us.

Another way I deal with anger is to talk to someone whom I trust who understands me. No, I do not mean another female friend who hates her body. That is not helpful. A bitchfest serves no one and can influence a spiral. I am only interested in talking about real feelings—the deep emotions I mentioned above, and having a safe space to dissect them. This is where my coaches and therapists have been ideal. They hold space for me and have made me unashamed to ask for help.

Early in my healing, the insanity going on in my head was unbearable. The barrage of thoughts about my body and food was maddening. The more I tried to stop it, the angrier I became. I'd ruminate for days, making my brain a miserable place to be.

On one particularly dark night of the soul, I finally confessed to my boyfriend how badly I was suffering. He listened, loved me, and supported me to find a therapist. My courage to ask for help was met with kindness and compassion.

I learned that by finding my way into the safe arms of a loved one, or to the office of a trustworthy professional, I could defuse the tension and anxiety that overwhelmed me.

More often than not, my therapist reminded me about the benefit of getting back into my body. *Walking, running, dancing, moving, breathing, feeling.* Allowing hard feelings to surface and using the energy they brought up to fuel my *movement.*

On a somatic level, our body can bury difficult emotions. By intentionally releasing these emotions, they can no longer remain stuck. It's a cathartic way to release anger and sadness.

Below is a simple, yet powerful four-step practice I can always count on when I'm feeling out of sorts:

1. Take a moment to set a clear intention. Something like: This practice is to release the anger at myself that I have gained five pounds.

2. Give your body permission to release: Sweet Body, I allow you to release any unprocessed anger, sadness, and stress that remains here.

3. Then move it, my friend! Dance, shake, rattle, and roll.

4. While your heart is beating hard, connect with yourself, and allow the energy to leave your body. Having a movement practice to support the release of your feelings is imperative.

Don't expect anger to be released every time you go for a run or exercise unless you explicitly set an intention around it. Trust me, I did all the overexercising in the world. It did not have the same effect as consciously stepping or dancing it out.

Movement allows you to stay out of the stories of what made you angry, and go straight for the dense emotions that remain in your tissues: anger, upset, frustration—all fuel.

Finding ways to be with these feelings in a productive way will guide you to more freedom. It's unbelievable how many of us go through our whole life not knowing how to process anger effectively. But being a good friend means being a good listener—especially in times of conflict. Especially when we are absorbing something we don't want to hear. So, let me ask you: *Can you hold space for yourself in a moment of anger?* I implore you to try, intend, and get moving!

14

Be of Service

"I don't know what your destiny will be, but one thing I
know: the only ones among you who will be really happy
are those who have sought and found how to serve."
– Albert Schweitzer

One of my first conscious lessons that stilled my body obsessions was becoming someone of service. It feels like a random suggestion until you try it. I love to take the focus off myself by asking,

Who needs me right now?

Is there a better way I could be spending my time?

What would be a resourceful place to put all this pent-up energy?

Where can I make a contribution?

These questions can help bring about an entirely new perspective. They can make our world seem more expansive and bring to light more important issues than,

What do I look like right now?

Does my butt look big in these pants?

Me, me, me!

Our action steps toward health can sometimes serve us the most when they have nothing to do with us, and everything to do with someone else. A cause isn't too hard to find. It can start in the home:

something as simple as folding laundry for your roommate or calling your neighbor who might be overdue for a good chat.

Being of service gets us out of a self-focused headspace, which can bring personal issues into perspective overall. My problems seem a lot smaller when I'm talking to a friend in need or adding people to my long-distance Reiki healing chain. The *what* doesn't matter as much as the *why*. And it's best if the why is personal—thus my dedication to helping women restore their relationships with their bodies. It's something that drives me on a spiritual level. It's my calling.

Science has proven that helping others reduces stress and ignites the same hormones that create happiness, bonding, and positive feelings. It increases oxytocin, dopamine, and releases serotonin—our pleasure hormones. The same hormones that get released during sex can be ours just by helping others. It also infuses our life with purpose and helps us create new goals that are not focused on our food intake or body size. This can create a positive ripple effect in our lives that makes us more content all around. [14]

There are people far less fortunate than ourselves—and far more interesting—with whom we can build community. They might open up our lives, and teach us about that which we've never experienced. Robbing ourselves of this opportunity to expand mentally, emotionally, and spiritually isn't worth it. Staying trapped in the house, obsessing about the last slice of cake we ate, will only rob us of the precious hours we could have spent being a better friend to ourselves by being of service to others. I see this a lot in my clients; one that specifically comes to mind is Brena.

Brena was *so* upset at herself. She felt so confident and excited about her newfound freedom with food. Until—she stepped on the scale. She thought she had lost weight but had actually gained two pounds. *Oh,*

---

14   *Publications.* Mental Health Foundation. (n.d.). Retrieved January 10, 2022, from https://www.mentalhealth.org.uk/explore-mental-health/publications/ doing-good-altruism-and-wellbeing-age-austerity. http://sitn.hms.harvard.edu/ flash/2017/love-actually-science-behind-lust-attraction-companionship/.

mama! She was pissed.

Brena ranted and raved. "How can I feel so good in my body, confident at work and full of energy AND have gained weight?"

I let her get out all the upset and then gave her a task. "Go help a neighbor for one hour!"

Confused, she asked, " What does helping my neighbor have to do with my weight and feelings?"

She was about to find out. I nudged her to lean in and give it a try—and . . . she listened.

Later that week, Brena went across the street to the elderly couple and offered to clean up their messy yard. And you guessed it—she called me a few days later, thrilled that she couldn't have cared less about her weight and focused more on feeling good. Finally, she was back to feeling great in her body!

That's why service is *so* interwoven into my message! Love Your Body Love Yourself, is all about service. When searching for a solution to share with others, I purposefully step out of the problem. When I have hit a wall with my body or food, I often think, *What would I tell a client?*

When I step into the role of being in service to another, I become of service to myself. That's what BE-Friending ourselves is all about. Then, I'll share a post on Instagram and Facebook to help anyone else with a similar issue. I don't sit alone in my pain forever. I have allowed my struggle to become my service. Therein, writing this book has been a powerful act of service that has helped me heal and kept me on track. Seriously, YOU are helping me right now. By reading this book, I have learned and have grown tremendously—and I am so grateful!

15

Be Moved

"My grandmother started walking five miles a day when
she was sixty. She's ninety-seven now, and we
don't know where the heck she is."
– *Ellen DeGeneres*

The summer after I graduated from college, I was invited to tour
nationally, performing musical theater and murder mysteries. There
were four of us driving all over the country in a cramped minivan. Sitting
on my butt for several hours per day made me crazy; as a result, this is
when my unhealthy relationship with food evolved into a full-fledged
eating disorder. I was consumed by the fear that I wasn't moving my
body enough and felt trapped by just sitting there, with no way to burn
calories. So, I did what any body-obsessed girl would do. I lived on
frozen yogurt and baby food from gas stations and worked out at any
possible given moment.

No one ever knew how tired I was after long nights on the bathroom
floor of hotels. During the day, I'd drink laxative tea, then be left with
an upset stomach that had me writhing and cramping on the cold tile in
between pooping my brains out. By morning, I'd pass it off, like nothing
happened. Put makeup on, and drink caffeine—hoping it'd reverse my
terrible night bender.

Mornings during tour were the perfect time to privately torture myself. Because part of this insane addiction to self-abuse . . . is getting away with *hiding* it. On occasion, after a long night of performing and driving, I woke up at an obscene hour to hit the gym before we left for our next gig. While running, I fell asleep on the treadmill—literally fell asleep. I fell off the treadmill. Crashed and burned, I lay on the floor with my whole right side bruised. This happened because I feared sitting in a van all day, gaining weight from not exercising. I got off easy. I only had some bruises when I could have had a broken arm.

The universe gave me these gracious wake-up calls along the way. Unfortunately, I struggled for many more years before I could even acknowledge that I had a problem. The determination to be thin made me overlook the obvious red flags; I had tunnel vision, and the warning signs went unseen.

I have always loved to exercise, dance, and move my body. However, as I planted my butt in that van, obsessing over my appearance, disordered eating became the axis of my life. Everything from getting dressed, to nourishing my body, to exercise was agony—I ended up using ways to care for myself against me. I became an exercise bulimic. If I overate, then I would exercise compulsively to work it off. I wouldn't eat certain foods unless I knew I had time to hit the gym or walk up and down my five-floor apartment building a dozen times. My mind was always tracking: *calories in, calories out.*

If I overate, then I had to beat myself up. My weapon was exercise fueled by self-criticism. This was my ritual. I thought by walking on an internal tightrope constantly, I could teach myself discipline.

Early on, I met a woman named Katie, who had a story similar to my own. She shared how she missed out on her life by exercising for hours a day, that she'd watch people walk by the gym at her college, laughing with their friends and having fun, while she beat herself up, in isolation, on the treadmill. She was—confidently—twenty pounds heavier than me, and it scared me to death. I was afraid that if I stopped exercising, I would gain weight like her.

One day, I ate more pizza than I had planned. My belly was full, and I was in utter disgust with my never-ending lack of control. I sat in my living room with the glaring truth that if I wanted to heal, I could not go for a run or the gym. I had to sit with the food in my belly. It was excruciating and uncomfortable. I called Katie and shared with her that I felt like I was going to die, that it felt like my life was ending. Sure, I've always been a drama queen, but this was sincerely scary for me. Katie didn't even say much. She simply listened to my feelings and agreed that *it sucks*. And somehow—through her simple act of hearing me, I survived the moment. To my relief, I didn't gain twenty pounds on-site. These moments of truth are what helped me to recover.

I faced my fears by trusting that I could get through the pain. What I never expected was that more pleasure was awaiting me on the other side.

Pleasure in living.

Pleasure in relationships.

Pleasure in indulging.

Pleasure in exercise.

Pleasure in enjoying fruits and veggies.

Pleasure in bed.

This pleasure only came by learning to listen to myself and my body. To comply when it said:

Slow down.

Take a nap.

Don't go for a run.

In the beginning, I didn't want to listen to that *nonsense*. But slowly, I began to open up to the idea that healing meant becoming partners with my body. If my body wanted to move, I moved. If it needed protein, I nourished it. If it craved hydration, I drank water. I became my own best friend by stretching and breathing deeply when my body was too tired for an exercise class. This was pivotal in my healing.

My relationship to exercise is something that continues to mend. I have grown too accustomed to pushing my body continually. Now, I work to keep my ambition in check. While I like to loosely plan my workout the night before, my priority is to listen to my body. Being a best friend to myself means I check in with Marla before doing anything strenuous. My mind may have ideas, but my body runs the show. For example, if I go to bed planning on doing a home workout with Olaf, but then wake up feeling sleepy, I don't push myself to make it happen.

Additionally, I have even stopped thinking of it as *exercise*. Instead, I think of it as *giving my body movement. Movement*, for me, looks different from day to day.

Because of my old, addictive behavior to exercise, I, to this day, have to check in and make sure I'm not exercising for weight loss. A good friend holds you accountable, and so, I am accountable to myself. I do my best to exercise solely for the joy and benefits of connecting with myself in movement.

I am intentional to begin every period of movement slowly. I get quiet with myself, and ease into it, breathing deeply, feeling all the places that are speaking, while I stretch and sigh into each position. I let my body guide me rather than forcing it. While I continue to tap into what my body wants, it will sometimes suggest,

Let's go for a walk.

Dance it out.

How about some yoga?

My only responsibility at that point is to honor it—and *that's* where the real discipline comes in; it's all about putting intention and consistency into the places that serve you. These conversations with my body have been key; self-dialogue has been integral to my removing force from my movement routine.

For years, I was my body's worst nightmare. I told it how long, fast, and hard to run. I didn't listen when it said,

Please slow down.

As a result of not listening, I was plagued by minor injuries, illness, and lethargy. It had the last word. Through trial and error, I have found that I can connect to my body and find my pleasure.

On vacation in Maui, I took a hardcore fitness class. As part of my recovery, I didn't take those classes for years, because it triggered my exercise-bulimic brain. I cared more about my sanity than the size of my butt. Now, I can occasionally take a class for fun; my mind no longer spins with

How are you going to keep this up?

If you lose weight from taking this class, then you will always have to take this class.

You aren't strong enough for this anymore.

You look like a fool.

At the time of that specific class, I thought I was past those thoughts. I was discouraged at their determination to creep back in, which is common in those who have overcome exercise addiction. Adamant about preserving my sanity, I sat quietly in my car, and let myself process the feelings I was having during the class. It would have been easy to fly by these emotions; I was on vacation, so there was even more of an excuse to not examine them. But my continual recovery depends on slowing down the tapes inside my head and listening to that scared little girl voice inside of me *speak*:

When we workout that hard I feel scared and sad.

I don't want to do this anymore.

I want to go home and lie down.

Can't we rest?

I feel overwhelmed by this.

I am ready to leave.

She was triggered by the exercise class and didn't feel safe. It wasn't fun *for her*. Just by being present, and willing to hear her, my body relaxed. I was able to notice where most of those thoughts aren't real. In turn, I was able to bring myself back to a mental sobriety where I could sort through my core wounds around movement. And let's be clear, this slowing down to be with myself took about seven minutes, less time than it takes to add to your Instagram story. Healing doesn't have to be laborious or consume every hour of every day, it's *baby steps*; it's how we engage ourselves while we're standing in front of the mirror or preparing our morning smoothie.

While working with my clients, I've realized, there's the other ex-treme—where people despise exercising. They disconnect from their bodies. They hate working out, and it brings up dissatisfaction for them to have to *move*.

My client Tim had a litany of excuses on why exercise didn't work for him. Like many people, *I don't have enough time* was Tim's core belief. His life was bustling with family matters and work obligations. Tim was not willing to prioritize exercise. But his body kept underscoring the reality that he needed it. With sluggish energy, low back pain, and irritability, he came to me for help. Tim knew that beating himself up at the gym or working with a trainer wouldn't be sustainable long-term. It never had in the past, and he was looking for a complete mental rewiring of his relationship with exercise.

I suggested Tim stop referring to moving his body as "exercise." When he made that simple adjustment, he was able to relate to his body differently. We worked to ease him into it. He set a timer for ten minutes and began to move his body slowly, knowing he had to start somewhere, and being gentle with himself, even when it felt like walking through sludge.

Tim created his own movement regime. Writing his own routine made him feel empowered and more connected to his body than my giving him a practice. It began with ten pushups, ten sit-ups, and ten squats. After that, he was *done*. Then, feeling accomplished, Tim could celebrate that he opened his body up with breath and movement. Slowly, he worked up to twenty reps per day, then fifty. Most of the battle was overcoming his negative thoughts:

This will never work.

It's only ten minutes, so it doesn't count.

If I miss a day. I might as well quit.

There's no way I'll keep this up long-term.

Over time, Tim found he was looking forward to his movement regime. It expanded into thirty minutes and a long walk after work. His methods of exercise expanded, not because he was pushing himself, but because he craved it.

An important question I ask my clients to consider:

What is my exercise story?

I didn't even realize my exercise had become dysfunctional until it was far too late—even when I fell asleep on the treadmill. This is where I tell my clients to do some journaling and consider their relationship to movement over the years. I ask them things such as

Do you push yourself even when you know you need to rest?

Do you exercise to beat yourself up because you feel you ate too much?

Do you exercise in the all or nothing mentality?

Do you avoid movement at all costs?

Writing it all down can be helpful, because they are able to see how their process evolves.

My friend Ella hated working out. A couple of times a year, she would get all gung ho about a new exercise plan. She would convince herself that fitness was her newfound obsession. She'd go all in, hot and heavy, kick-starting her plan with a boot camp that lasted for two weeks. During that time, Ella would push herself, override her edges, and eventually hurt herself.

Her injury was a perfect excuse to stop and go back to her no-exercise routine. Instead of finding something that was enjoyable and sustainable, she banged herself around. This became a noticeable pattern that demonstrated unhealthy patterns in her relationship with movement.

Do you have this pattern?

Do you see it around you?

We love to push past our limits, burn out, blame it on exercise, then stop. It is a vicious cycle that leads to stagnation and disconnection with our bodies. When we find a way to make movement fun or even neutral, we can continually show up for ourselves in a new way.

Consider your excuses for too much or not enough exercise. What are the things that you're telling yourself that is keeping you from moving your body? One of my favorite quotes from Sakyong Mipham reads:

The body benefits from movement, and the mind benefits from stillness.

We must have both. Think of it like meditation. The longer we stay in stillness, the deeper we can go. Once we find a movement that feels right, our body will thrive. Even if we have an injury or illness, we can find ways to activate the body in a gentle way that supports ourselves. It can be challenging to find a movement practice that works. Many people throw away any idea of exercising. If you want to see a movement that works, with attention and care, it is possible.

An integral part of this practice is expanding the horizon for what exercise can *be*. Did you play sports as a child? Would a game of soccer still be fun? What about dancing to rock 'n' roll for a couple of songs, going for a walk, lifting dumbbells, or watching yoga on YouTube? There's nothing I love more than learning about what my best friends like *to do* for fun. How would you like to get moving with your best friend?

We can get stuck on thinking that exercise means going to the gym or taking an aerobics class. For some, that can be an excellent structure. For others, it feels lifeless or uncomfortable. The point is to find a way to make moving your body enjoyable.

Lisa hated exercising.

"Marla, I hate it. I hate sweating. There's nothing I like about it. But I do know that my pain of not exercising is bigger than the pain of doing it," she said.

After a few sessions together, Lisa was able to mend her relationship with movement by focusing on all the benefits that exercise gives her. Her *aha!* moment was realizing when weight loss was her motivation for exercise, her willpower faded quickly.

When she wasn't seeing results quickly enough, or blew her diet due to emotional eating, she'd say *screw it*. When Lisa focused on why it was good for her well-being, she was far more willing to stick it out. She recognized diet and exercise are closely related—if her diet went down the drain, so did her exercise. By showing up for herself, day after day, she was able to learn what she actually enjoyed. She walked, lifted weights, did yoga, and stretched. Soon, Lisa began to like it—*no, not love it*, but her body found its groove.

She made a list that supported the benefits of exercise and hung it up in her bathroom. Every time she wavered, I'd guide her back to her list. As she reminded herself daily of why she wanted to exercise, she began to integrate into her mind and body.

Weight loss became obsolete.

Let's make a list of all the ways exercise is good for our bodies from a health standpoint.

It releases toxins.

It increases circulation.

It gives us energy and makes us feel alive.

It helps us be more confident.

It helps us sleep better.

Why do you like to move your body? Why do you exercise? How would moving daily benefit you?

Here is a list to inspire you:

1. I want to have the energy for my children.

2. I want to be able to run around the backyard with my grandchild.

3. My family has a history of heart disease; I want my heart to be healthy.

4. I had breast cancer, and exercise is crucial to my health.

5. Quite simply, I feel good after I exercise.

For me, going beyond exercise helped me stay motivated. It was about slowing down. For you, it may be about picking it up—that's okay too, just be honest about your intentions. Trust that your body has innate wisdom that will teach you how and when to move. Trust creates a connection and friendship with our body that will grow. When we work with ourselves rather than against ourselves—we will *thrive*.

Diet culture mentality will get us on the momentous wheel of exercising a lot, and getting our food *on track*. Then, when we feel like we're finally getting a weight loss breakthrough—what happens? We usually hit resistance of some kind. Maybe it's a plateau, or maybe our body gets sick. While most fitness coaches say to push past this point, I propose it's better to *slow down or even stop*. Why? Well, I personally believe that's our body's way of protecting us.

Lindo Bacon's *Health at Every Size*[15] presents us with scientific research around dieting and how our body can go into survival mode if we push it too much. It will create resistance and issues that keep us from enjoying our body. We can notice this is happening if we begin to feel overly lethargic. I don't know how many times I thought to myself, *I was on a good roll here. I was doing great with my food; exercising really hard, but now I'm sick, and I just don't want to.* And it's because my body was being a good friend to me. Most of the time, we think we are sabotaging ourselves or doing something wrong. The more we tune into what our body wants and needs, the more we'll be on the right track to looking and feeling fantastic.

---

15   Lindo Bacon PhD, *Health At Every Size: The Surprising Truth About Your Weight*, lindobacon.com, 2023, lindobacon.com/health-at-Every-Size-Book.

16

Belong

"Those who have a strong sense of love and belonging
have the courage to be imperfect."
– *Brené Brown*

I am a bright girl. I got all As in high school, graduated Magna Cum Laude in College, was an enthusiastic learner, and have historically been *happy* throughout my life. And yet, I had this huge blind spot around how to properly care for my body. Sure, I'd read books on it. But nothing resonated, and nothing stuck.

I believed I had two primary issues:

My body wasn't thin enough.

I couldn't control my food intake.

I believed once I had these two problems resolved, I could enjoy my life. Until then, my mission was to fix this awful situation that I was cruelly given.

In turn, I used my body and food as my coping mechanism for everything. Bingeing. Restricting. Overexercising. Food obsession. I had no idea how to be a good friend to myself at the time. It took years to realize that my issues had *nothing* to do with my body, nor did they have to do with my food intake. My issues began and ended in my mind.

It's true. I compulsively ate and used exercise to control my weight.

It's also true that when left alone, cleaning up the dishes at a dinner party, I would likely eat another meal or two off of people's plates. It was all about gaining and losing control. Obsessing over food and my body was the only coping mechanism I had.

It was easier to lament about eating too much than to feel the fear of a love interest not calling me back. *No need to go to that audition, I am too big for that role anyway.* Easier to blame it on my body than to take responsibility for my fear of rejection.

You may be thinking the same thing. *My life is good other than the fact that my jeans from high school don't fit, and I can't stop eating cookies at night.*

However, these issues are a matter of fixation, and have nothing to do with the real, internal reasons we binge or diet. The discomfort and anguish around our body is an emotion we can be aware of. I understand this is challenging to consider, as we often feel as though we don't get a decision in the way we feel. Either way, we certainly have a choice in how we react. Do we sit with the discomfort of having an argument with our partner? Do we stuff a couple dozen cookies down our throats?

The energy we bring to our recovery is the result we receive. It's difficult to be present with ourselves; it can feel scary to stare down our triggers—*and gosh! Can they feel like demons!* However, those places inside of us that are experiencing tremendous pain are actually begging for love and compassion. When I want to crawl out of my own skin with discomfort, I give myself time to *be* with difficult feelings.

So, what does that look like?

I begin by closing my eyes and taking a deep breath. I address myself with tenderness, the way I would with a best friend who needs hugs and compassion. That's what we get to do for ourselves. I would sit with her and let her cry it out and feel upset without wanting to change her or make it better. Being in the moment with ourselves allows us to release the emotion and expectation that we are always supposed to feel *good*.

It has been through my experience that I am best able to sit with myself and feel through meditation. If you are wondering why meditation is important, connecting and tending to ourselves–without the need to *fix it*–is one benefit. So . . . take three minutes to breathe if that's all you can do, then expand it to five . . . then fifteen. It will become easier over time as you establish a sense of trust with yourself.

In college, I was cheating on my boyfriend with this really sexy actor. We both were unfaithful. Every time I saw his girlfriend, I felt tremendous shame. And I could hardly make eye contact with my boyfriend. When I look back at pictures of myself during this time, I see a slightly plump Marla who was eating to bury her feelings of guilt.

This rebellion against being a constant good girl was exhilarating, but my negative feelings had me overeating and bingeing late at night. Was it the food's fault?

Nope. It was the only way I knew *to cope*. I learned early on in recovery that my relationship with food and my body had a spiritual solution. I came to understand whenever I turned to food, I could turn to God instead. I could call upon something greater than myself to soothe my pain. After all, food never soothed the ache for long, and my relationship with Spirit has seen me through. While tools help, there is a component of healing that is solely surrender. Without the sovereign hand of a higher helper, I would be shouldering a load I don't have the stamina to carry.

According to Abraham Maslow's hierarchy of needs, the sense of *belonging is part of one of his major needs that motivate human behavior.*
[16] So, to tell ourselves it *doesn't matter* if we're on the receiving end of rejecting behaviors is to deny a fundamental base need and to lie to ourselves. It matters because reciprocity in relationships matters, love matters, community matters, and feeling peace in connection matters. So then, what do we do when our issues surrounding food do what they do best (isolate us from other people, and create unnecessary

16   https://www.verywellmind.com/what-is-the-need-to-belong-2795393

competition with other women)? Well, the last thing we need to do is shame ourselves for it.

It is imperative to acknowledge the part of ourselves that feels separate and scared, and to nurture it. We must give ourselves full permission to cry, pound our fists, fight back, or collapse beneath the weight of our feelings. Then, we *must* take our power back, and consider new ways to build strong connections in this life.

If your partner pulls back their love because of your belly, hips, or thighs, then maybe it's time to look for a new partner, who doesn't hesitate to tell you how beautiful you are.

If your husband doesn't like your post baby body, let him have his process, but be clear about where you stand. He may be projecting his fears about letting go of the life before baby.

I acknowledge these things can be challenging—excruciating even, and might create their own period of complicated emotions and grief, but by facing difficult realities, we build a strong relationship with the truth, and can stand in our own experience in a more empowered way. Living integral to our truth, and seeing ourselves through the discomfort of doing so, is living authentically. I personally don't like hanging out with disingenuous people. If we are BE-Friending ourselves, the foundation of that relationship must be honesty.

Friends who only focus on their bodies, polishing selfies, and curating their diets can be a drag. Trust me there are other tribes and friends that don't need physical recognition to feel safe. I challenge you to find them! Explore your environment! You might find friends who have the same orientation to wellness as you, and these relationships are invaluable.

While there is certainly an element that is outside of our control when it comes to matters of belonging, we can set standards that create a safe space for ourselves and communicate to others the type of love we are looking to receive.

By treating ourselves with radical compassion, and being our own bestie, we can better screen those applying for the job of *friend*. Becoming the template of how we want to be treated makes it easier to filter out relationships that do not fulfill us, or might drain us long term. Part of *belonging* is determining where you *don't want to fit in*. Let's strive to not fit with those who only sow and reap negativity and self-criticism.

My client Sheila is a tall, beautiful basketball player with legs for days. Still, she came to me, wrestling with her appearance. She needed to know she was beautiful. Every day, she fought with her inner critic who would constantly berate her:

They don't think you are beautiful.

You look ugly today.

You are looking too good; they are going to be uncomfortable and judge you.

When she was going out, looking fabulous, with her hair done up, and wearing a crop shirt, her mother would immediately chime in with "Oh, you look too good. What will others say? Don't you think you should change your clothes?"

On top of her beauty, which made her feel separate from others, she was an introvert, and liked to be quiet. However, she found that if she was silly, goofy, and the life of the party, others were more comfortable with her beauty, and this made her feel safe. The problem was that this pattern kept her moving further and further away from authenticity. She was beautiful and shy. Yet she felt alone. We found a voice inside her that said,

If I am beautiful I will be alone.

If I am myself, others won't accept me.

We set out on an experiment that encouraged her to stretch past her discomfort and lean into her natural inclinations. If she was at a party, she allowed herself to be quiet and listen. She would go out with her boyfriend, looking like a model, and let her mom be uncomfortable about it. By taking these actions, she began to show that scared part of herself that it was indeed *safe*. She also let herself sit in the feelings of being quiet when she felt someone was judging her. By sitting through the complicated feelings, they began to dissolve.

We cannot grow until we allow ourselves to feel more deeply. Feeling our emotions is key to freedom of self.

How we speak to ourselves is the most fundamental to becoming our own best friend … If you are constantly putting yourself down and calling yourself names, feeling good is not in the cards for you. So, I'm here to tell you to *snap out of it!* Because . . . that's what my mom would say. (Stay tuned for more on *snapping out of it*, and my mother's brilliant advice.)

These voices that are telling us that we aren't good enough, smart enough, thin enough, strong enough, or _____enough are actually scared and wanting to keep us safe.

Let's take Shelia as an example. Her voice that was telling her she wasn't beautiful enough was making sure that she felt safe, because remember: *if she was beautiful then no one would like her.* Often, these strong incessant voices are a smoke screen for deeper feelings; discerning the message beyond the message can be challenging and enriching.

My obsessive thoughts about food occupied my mind. They were better than grappling with my feeling like a failure in my acting career. Believing I *wasn't thin enough* was safer than dealing with my discomfort around fighting with my husband.

Feeling bad about myself became my comfort zone. I knew *too well* how to be the sassy friend who has nothing nice to say to myself. In turn, learning what was beneath my beliefs was a new liaison.

Discovering what was beneath my belief about my arms being too big, my thighs being too flabby, or my cheeks being too plump was complicated in the beginning. The important thing to remember is that not all voices of fear are villains; while their language is full of lies, their primary goal is to keep us protected—a wild paradox, I know.

The more I slowed down, the more I began to understand their intentions. I'd ask myself, *Oh Marla, are you okay? It seems you are upset about something. You keep being so mean to yourself.*

Then I'd hear a voice inside myself saying, *Yes, I am scared. I feel out of control. I am afraid people will judge me and reject me.* This internal dialogue gave me something to work with. By encouraging myself to peel back the layers, I was able to uncover what was really fueling the cycles that were not serving me.

I get it. It sounds crazy to have conversations with yourself, but the reality is, we're all doing it, all the time, anyway. There's a voice inside your head that is constantly jabbering away about something. This is your opportunity to write a script that will help you feel better. In fact, I encourage my clients to sit down and think about the ways they would encourage a best friend going through their primary issues. One of my favorite exercises is to write a letter to myself, and build myself up the way I would a girlfriend.

Dear Marla,

You're gorgeous. You're worthy. You're valuable. I love you. I'm sorry I haven't been kind to you. From now on, I will have your back no matter what. Above all things, I want you to know you don't have to strive. You're allowed to rest. You're allowed to take up space. You're allowed to belong, exactly as you are.

Sincerely,

Your Best Friend

Okay, your turn!

17

Be Sane

"Snap out of it!"
– *My mom*

The mornings at the Mervis house were a wardrobe nightmare. My sister Jill and I shared a room, a pantry-sized bathroom, a closet, and the clothes inside. With shirts, skirts, pants, and blouses strewn everywhere, we'd lament at each other and say things like, "You are wearing the shirt that matches my skirt! Please! This shirt makes me look awful! Give me yours! I can't believe you're not going to let me have that; you're *trying* to make me look bad! You're terrible!"

You know—all that good *sister stuff*.

The tragedy of wearing something to school that made me look dumpy or wasn't *cool* would put me in tears.

"Really?!" My mom would say, "Snap out of it! You look fine. Get out of here, or you will be late for school!"

Good on ya, Mom. *Snap out of it.*

I didn't realize how challenging it would be to raise three daughters until I was in my twenties. The amount of estrogen and drama that my poor mom and dad had to deal with must have been overwhelming.

Snap out of it! was a common phrase my mom would say to keep my sisters and me from teetering off the ledge. Granted, I didn't always love it. Sometimes I felt invalidated, and responded like the reactive teenage girl I was, but as a coach, I've learned the value of *Snap out of it!* and that it can be good, when integrated appropriately and in the confines of safety.

The rules are: you've gotta be your own best friend about it; that means you must take time to hear yourself, feel your feelings, and support your position.

Our inner children need to feel validated *before* we can institute something as sassy as this mantra, which can arguably restore us to momentary sanity. The goal is to sit with the feelings. Never shut them up; listen, meditate in love . . . then get *real* with ourselves through calling our minds into the present.

It's okay for your inner voice to get a little bit sassy. We all have that fiery best friend who levels with us when we take it a little bit too far. There are situations that absolutely *call* for her voice to show up.

For example, I truly think department store mirrors are a conspiracy designed to make women entirely delusional. 360-degree mirrors placed under fluorescent lighting would make *any* person want to cover every square inch of their body in clothing. This is how they hook us into walking away from the register with bags on each arm; there's *truly* no better place to *Snap out of it!* than a poorly lit, department store dressing room!

Or what about right before an event, when you're perfecting your makeup, and agonizing over that last-minute stress zit on your nose? Though any sane person would tell you, *No one will ever notice that!* It's the one small thing that sends you spiraling. In these cases, *just snap out of it!* is the smelling salt you need to shake you awake and remind you that you *deserve* a fun night out, without the absurdity of worrying about a microscopic pimple.

Snap out of it—don't go there.
Snap out of it—pull back!
Snap out of it—don't say that.
Snap out of the pits of despair.

Stop the negative talk before it takes you on a downward spiral. Afterall, what good friend would abandon her bestie at such a moment?

Being able to reign in our minds at the snap of a finger can work wonders *if* we can do it honorably. So, if you're spinning out, feel free to bookmark this page, and turn to it, if ever you need a reminder to *Snap out of it!*

In high school, I used to vacation with a handful of my best girlfriends every summer, on Rehoboth Beach. I saved my money year-round for the occasion—I loved a shopping spree! One year, I was thrilled to find a short, skimpy, dress at my favorite store on the main strip. Sadly, the last size of this sexy dress was one size too small for me. Still, *I wanted to buy it!*

My brutally honest friend took one look at me, trying to zip up the dress, and offered me another option.

"Oh, don't worry, I plan on losing seven pounds and fitting into this in a month," I said, with chocolate ice cream stains on my chin, and all down my shirt. My friend shrugged and left me in the dressing room alone to stare at myself in the mirror. As I stood there, observing myself in silence, I suddenly didn't feel so great about the dress.

Doing what it does best, my brain turned against me. Anxiety and dark thoughts about my body raced through my mind: *I am dumpy, ugly, and . . . my friend agrees. In fact, she's left me here . . . to prove a point!*

Lies.

As I continued to lose touch with reality, a mother walked by my dressing room with her three children. The middle one was wiggling around, having a major tantrum, screaming at the top of his lungs. The eldest one was pulling on her mom's arm, pleading to check out the toy store. The infant, in the stroller, was starting to cry from all the commotion.

"Do you need some help?" I asked, kindly.

Without waiting for a response, I stepped out of the stall, picked up the baby, and started talking to the eldest child about her favorite toys.

This gave the mother time to deal with her son, who was attempting to take all his clothes off. It was every parent's nightmare.

After the woman soothed her son, I placed her infant back into her arms. And everything was right as rain. Soon, the woman thanked me, and we parted ways.

I glanced down, realizing I was still wearing the tiny dress; in the midst of the commotion, I had somehow forgotten. I marveled at how quickly everything had happened. Only moments before, I was miserable and ready to crawl under a rock. Now, I was happily singing the "Rainbow Connection" from the Muppets. My mood shifted rapidly from palpable torture to complete ease, and I realized: the spirit of my mother was in that place.

She was there, saying *Marla! Snap out of it!*—*inviting* me out of my head, and back into the present, where I belonged.

Now, the most integral part of using this mantra is our personal dissection of our core negative beliefs. It never entirely works unless the lies you've told yourself for years are debunked and replaced with truths. That whirlwind of lies is the *IT* we're snapping out of.

My *IT* consisted of negative feelings about my body, and an inability to see my own worth. It took me time to recognize the best part of that memory was my willingness to be kind, and help another person. *That loving girl was me. That was Marla. That was the truth about myself I needed to believe.*

So, I challenge you to consider: what is the *IT* you need to snap out of? Is it lies about your appearance? Your worth? Your work as a creative, professional, or parent? Your abilities? Whatever your *IT* is, know that the sooner you correct your core beliefs, the more easily you can come back to yourself during intense moments of anxiety and shame.

Once you understand your own power, and allow self-advocacy to filter out the lies you're believing, you can

Snap out of it!

And snap back into a state of sanity and celebration of your own brilliance!

18

Be Forgiven

"Forgiveness is not an occasional act, it is a constant attitude."
– *Martin Luther King Jr.*

When I took my first delicious bite of freedom in my thirties, I couldn't help but glance back at my past in remorse. I was immediately struck with the realization of how I'd missed out on years of countless joyful moments in my life because I'd been so concerned about my weight. In turn, it felt like an anvil had landed on my chest. Ashamed of my actions, anger arose from my belly. How could I have been so vain?

I'd been so consumed with my appearance that I didn't get to enjoy indulgences with my friends; feel the "spark" of getting all dressed up; or experience full physical pleasure with my partners. How could I care so much about my caloric intake that I'd skip out on dinner with a friend? How could I let fear of weight gain push me into exhausting exercise?

Mean words, awful words . . . which I am not going to write here, were in my mind and on my lips. When I get this low (and I still do), I reach out for support from my friends or my mentor. As I went to dial my best friend's number, I stopped and chose to self-soothe. After all, I needed to be my own best friend, and suddenly, when I leaned in to listen to my own pain, it hit me: If I was going to continue my healing journey, I needed to forgive myself.

What a hard pill to swallow knowing that forgiveness was the answer. While it's easy to forgive other people, giving myself that same grace wasn't my jam.

Let's be honest, my disordered eating pattern was fueled by self-punishment. I wouldn't forgive myself for gaining weight after being sick, or even when I didn't get the baby weight off "fast enough." In turn, I'd fall back into binge eating after months and months of progress. Situation after situation would happen where forgiveness was out of the question. Too often, I see my clients experiencing the same emotions and cycles.

Take Jackie, for example:

Jackie couldn't forgive herself when she'd had an evening of emotional eating. Though she was experiencing stress at work, she wouldn't lower the bar for herself in any regard. She expected perfection, and anytime she spoke out of line, gained a pound, or made a professional mistake, she belittled herself. Add a night of binge eating to the picture, and she was overcome with self-flagellation.

"If a child was learning a new skill, would you scold him if he made a mistake and didn't always do it right?" I asked her.

"No, of course not. But my eating is disgusting and gross. I'm a grown adult and know that this type of eating is bad for me, and I should know better," Jackie spewed.

I should know better. My, how those offensive four words pack on shame! We want better for ourselves. We do know better. But what we don't acknowledge is that feeling good about ourselves takes time. The only way I have seen women change their relationships with their appearance is through practicing consistent compassion. Pardoning slipups stops the shame and incites understanding. And we deserve it. Not only that, mercy and forgiveness work! Punishing behavior for making a perceived mistake only adds to the pain.

Because healing isn't linear, we need to expect that old behaviors might rear their ugly heads and make room for them when they do.

For months, I would feel freedom and ease with my body, then from out of nowhere, negative thoughts would creep in:

Oh, I can't believe your belly looks like that!

Did you actually eat that bagel—with the size of your butt?

I was appalled. I *should* have known better—after all, I was "healed" . . . didn't that make me immune? False. I still hear that voice from time to time—but I know the way to move through it is by empathizing with myself and tolerating my thoughts with more compassion.

A good friend asks questions about our behavior:

Why would you think that about yourself?

What's present emotionally for you?

When I did the same thing for myself, I found that I could forgive and let it go. The more I practiced kindness toward myself, the more the mean thoughts went away. If you are wondering how you better implement the idea of being pain free which you learned in chapter 11, the practice of forgiveness is perfect.

Where do you not forgive yourself in your life? Have you made a mistake toward yourself or someone else and you aren't letting yourself off the hook? When we cannot forgive ourselves regularly and allow ourselves to be human, we project our dissatisfaction onto what we see in the mirror.

Take my client Paige, for example: Paige and I were working together on her issues with binge eating. By addressing her emotional issues that were leading to binge eating, she slowly let go of this behavior. Paige lost weight and was surprised to find this sudden weight loss, in and of itself, profoundly triggering. As we delved into these pain points, Paige began to recognize that the different numbers on the scale represented herself at different ages—specifically ages where something difficult had happened. For instance, Paige weighed a specific number at twenty-five years old when she'd gone through a heart-wrenching breakup. When the scale reflected that number back to Paige, her body remembered the sensation of being that size. As a result, she reverted to twenty-five years old in her mind, and her emotions mirrored those she'd felt at the time. After working through her emotional blockages, we found

Paige couldn't forgive herself for her past, and this lack of forgiveness created constriction in her mind and body. In turn, we worked through helpful exercises that I have used in my own life. It mirrors what I do when conflict arises with friends in my own life—when I'm the one who has made a mistake. If I ever get to a place where I think, *I messed up. I hurt my friend.*

I do my best to make amends—to reconcile differences. I make sure both friends feel heard and understood; I own what is mine to hold, and usually—both loved ones experience an eagerness to move on. These are the dynamics of healthy friendships; engaging in healthy conflict can make us even more potent. But . . . what about when that conflict is with ourselves? We often don't give ourselves that kind of grace, and we don't know how to forgive ourselves and move past things—primarily because no one ever taught us how to do so.

So, my question for you is, can you forgive yourself? I mean, really forgive yourself—as opposed to shoving it down and pretending like it didn't happen? Can you be present with your own pain, move past it, and have compassion for who you were when it happened? Can you forgive yourself the way you would forgive a friend?

There are things we've done in our lives that may feel irredeemable; many feel big but are actually relatively small in the grand scheme of things. The memories that keep us weighed down for years can be difficult to process because they become blurry, faded, and make less sense over time. These types of scenarios can be complicated if the other person is no longer in the picture—perhaps they've passed, it is no longer safe to reach out to them, or it doesn't make sense to verbalize an apology after all this time.

This is where letter writing and journaling come in handy; to process those painful regrets and put them on the page. Sometimes, a ceremony is warranted—buy flowers, set up a space for yourself, grab a blanket, a notebook, and a cup of tea. Sit by a fire, or on a patio, or near a body of water. Whatever it looks like for you to support yourself—find that space and be forgiven. Allow yourself to release the past.

Here is a personal example from my journal; if it resonates, feel free to use it as a template:

Dear Marla,

I'm sorry that I don't pay attention to you. I override your hunger cues and stuff you with food. I get so tired and stressed and listening to you feels more like a chore than anything.

I want to listen and honor you. I want to be on better terms with you. Please be patient with me as I learn how to slow down and process my feelings. I am figuring out how to deal with anxiety without hurting you.

I'm sorry. I promise that I will do my best. It won't be perfect, but my commitment is to be nicer to you.

Love, Marla

The most important part of this exercise is to acknowledge our why and create compassion around it. Especially if we were younger when these things happened—many of us truly didn't have the resources to relate healthfully!

In my teenage years, I didn't have the wisdom; I didn't have the life experience—I made mistakes, and that's okay; I can look at that part of my younger self with compassion. The second part of this exercise is journaling back to ourselves.

For me, this sounded like:

Dear Marla,

Thank you for your apology. I completely understand why you are struggling . . . Thank you for your commitment to love me. I have nothing but the utmost compassion for you. If you would allow me, I'd like to teach you about the love you deserve by forgiving you.

I fully accept your apology, and I am lucky to grow with you.

Love, Marla

After completing this exercise, I place my hand over my heart. As I self-soothe, I am patient with the emotions that come up, and I allow love to flow into the spaces of myself that were blocked. That latter part is essential—when we allow ourselves to stay blocked from our own forgiveness, we create a division within our own being. We cannot live in a house divided and expect to find peace. As we come into alignment with ourselves, we must support ourselves. When we feel tender, we must be extra gentle and friend ourselves.

As you work through the exercise, consider the following statements and apply them to your situation, especially when it becomes challenging, or things resurface:

I'm forgiven.

I release the shame.

I am human.

I made a mistake, and I release the story.

I admit I was wrong, and I apologize—I stop being hard on myself.

I am forgiven. By God. By the other person. By myself. I let this go.

I accept that there are consequences of my behavior. I also accept the things I have lost because I made a mistake.

I forgive myself. I let this go. I deserve good things even though I made a mistake. I forgive myself and give the rest to God. I actively choose, every day, to forgive myself.

Self-forgiveness is a choice. It may seem like it's not, while we wait for the emotions to go away and the upset feelings to dissipate. But we get to choose, and we get to decide how to speak to ourselves and give self-care in moments of distress. It is tragic to live in a loop of spiraling shame—to have a condemning thought throughout life that never lets us off the hook. While the initial process of self-forgiveness can be triggering, as we do the work, we find we're easier to love than we once believed. In the parts of ourselves where we feel the most ashamed, we might come to recognize the face of a

Lonely, scared, hurting,

Wonderful, redeemable

Friend.

19

Be Integrated

"We must look at them and turn the light on them, and
when we turn the light on them—they're no longer shadows,
they can become implemented into who we are."
– *Carl Jung*

I can honestly say that while I've done exceptional work around my body and food, I still notice behaviors from which I have not recovered. The more curious I became about these "sticky" behaviors, the more I opened my mind to various ways of addressing them. It wasn't until I found Carolyn Elliott's book, *The Existential Kink* that I could attribute these to my *shadow*. The theory of *the shadow* was originated by Carl Jung who believed we have separate, more primitive sides to our personality that we can usher into the light by embracing and engaging with them.[17]

In an effort to fully accept and integrate my shadow, I realized I would first have to meet her. One thing I learned about Shadow Marla is that she is very sneaky. She experiences a deep indulgence when she sneaks food she shouldn't have, especially when she could be caught. Her sneakiness is specifically centered around the core belief, "I'm bad!"

---

17   *Essential Secrets of Psychotherapy: What is the "Shadow"?* (n.d.). Retrieved January 10, 2022, https://www.psychologytoday.com/us/blog/evil-deeds/202101/essential-se-crets-psychotherapy-what-is-the-shadow.

I am delectably . . . bad!

Many women are people pleasers. They want to be good spouses, good moms, good professionals—good overall. This means there's no real safe place to stand up, act out, or be bad. But that *screw this* energy has to go somewhere, right? I think we can all say it's exhausting to try to be perfect. I'm sick of striving for perfection! In turn—I sneak.

When I was younger, my sisters would always say, "Everyone thinks Marla is the perfect little girl, but it's because they don't know the thing she does behind the scenes! She is clever—and sneaky!"

The truth is—they were completely right, and that behavior went into my relationship with food without my realizing it. Even with my son, Aspen, I think, *I don't want him to see me eating chocolate because then he's gonna want it!* I'm sure a lot of moms can relate to this. We have snack drawers—we hide things. In part, because we don't want to have to share—but for me, I craved being sneaky.

It'd be easy to make this behavior (and any other shadow behavior) *wrong*. But, I actually enjoy making it indulgent. When I sneak a snack, I tell myself, "Ooh—I'm so sneaky! Isn't this sneaky? Look at me! I'm bad. I'm not eating kale. I'm adding extra cheese! How naughty!"

It creates the same satisfaction of having a binge eating night with my best girlfriend. That *If she's having fun, I'm having fun too* feeling. What I've learned, by BE-Friending Shadow Marla, is that allowing myself to be satisfied through the craving usually makes it far less naughty. Because let's face it—after we have complete access to the thing that is *naughty* or taboo, we typically lose all desire for it.

It's like when you really want that guy or girl. Then they finally ask you out or even make you their girlfriend. Then suddenly the luster is lost. It's *not that big of a deal* because *they're not that great.*

For the most part, women are encouraged to constantly "be nice," and told, "don't be crazy." If we become emotional, we are told we are "too much." But when we don't allow ourselves to have these emotions, when we don't accept these parts of ourselves, we push our issues down and turn to coping behaviors.

We are allowed to be turbulent.
We're allowed to be happy.
We're allowed to be sad.
We're allowed to be jealous.
We're allowed to be calm.
We're allowed to be out of control.

Women have a full spectrum of messy, vibrant, beautiful emotions—all of them are valuable.

I have clients who come to me who say, "It feels like I'm eating my anger," when they have gone off on another emotional eating bender. The truth is—they are. And they have entirely forfeited the indulgence of being wholeheartedly pissed. Women have been taught to be measured in everything, which has robbed them of the opportunity of seeing their most taboo emotions in full force.

We all have that friend who is a little bit reckless. She's the girl who does and says what she wants and doesn't care what anyone else thinks—and when she makes a raucous scene, or dramatically dumps her partner, or spends way too much money on a pair of stilettos . . . we quietly celebrate with her. Even if we act shocked and don't praise her, we all kind of want to be her. Because she's in full embrace of her Shadow self.

The good news is, we can all be that friend—to ourselves. We can show up totally defiant when we eat that delicious cupcake with the chocolate mousse on top. We can revel in our angst while blaring edgy music and screaming at the top of our lungs. We can revel in the deep, gross, satisfaction we get when we oversleep, overspend, overeat, and totally *blow it*.

One of my clients who struggled with overworking often bartered for time in mischievous ways. Sasha would deliberately dawdle before her morning commute, and if she only had ten minutes before she needed to be at her desk—she'd make a pit stop to get a coffee.

"I don't know why I do it," she admitted. "It's got to be some form of self-sabotage."

"Sure," I responded. "Or it could be the deep satisfaction you get by being late, because . . . it's forbidden."

The more she sat on this the more she admitted—there were *many* perks to being late. It felt autonomous. It felt mischievous. It felt unbridled. It felt youthful. It felt free. As we continued our work together, I encouraged Sasha to facilitate this feeling in other ways that wouldn't compromise her job. I also told her to allow herself to ride the high of not being timely.

The more Sasha realized this was more of an internal issue (feeling as though she never had time for herself), the more she was able to integrate her shadow and appreciate the bestie inside herself that was beckoning her to be free.

We can demonstrate friendship toward ourselves when we celebrate the complex, messy, "unacceptable" parts of who we are. In many cases, the way to pull back the curtain to reveal this part of our personhood requires a mirror. This is when a friend, partner, therapist, coach, or energy worker comes in handy. Because the shadow is something that falls *behind* us—it is only when we can see our reflection that we have full perspective on how to address it. And learning about our shadows with someone safe is especially important because Carl Jung emphasizes, "Your subconscious gets everything that it wants."

You see, we are great manifesters. Everything in our subconscious materializes into the physical world. So, when we become friends with our shadow—we learn what the subconscious truly wants. This can become tricky and confusing to navigate alone. Because maybe our subconscious says:

I never have enough money.

No one sees me.

I can't get the weight off.

We always want to blame our experiences on other things, but truly—we enjoy watching these things come to life. It is more important to our primal mind to be correct about our assumptions than it is to make ourselves truly happy. So, if the subconscious says, *I can't find a job*—external circumstances adhere accordingly, and we find ourselves applying for every position we can get our hands on . . . but never actually getting an interview.

I know for me—I am deeply satisfied by helplessness. I love thinking, *what if I never get it right? No matter what I do, I fail. Look at me! Forever helpless. I don't know what I'm going to do!* Part of BE-Friending Shadow Marla has looked like allowing myself to sit in that thought reel and derive pleasure out of the state of feeling small.

It feels good to clench my body up in distress, because when every muscle is tight—it feels like I'm being held. The more I work with myself the more I realize I enjoy the feeling of constriction—so, caring for myself looks like tensing up my muscles, wrapping up in a ball, and holding myself to derive enjoyment out of that tension.

I say, "Okay! Here's helpless Marla. She's so small and little! She needs help. Someone help her!" Then I come to my own side as a dear friend—I am my own rescuer. This is how I work to integrate my *dark* and *light* side. It's like internal role playing where I can both be the damsel in distress, and the savior. I get to lose and win and feel great about it.

One of the areas I see my shadow self the most is with moral superiority. I mean, nothing is as satisfying as imposing my moral philosophy on others. When my husband and I are in an argument—I love being the *good* one—the *right* one. Because the reality is, I get something out of thoughts like *I'm so loving and amazing, and you're being so terrible to me. I'm good. You're bad.*

Anyone else with me on this? Logically, we don't say these things. But we play out the power dynamics all the same. We have a vibrant dance with anger, because most of us don't know how to process it. I'd even wager sometimes we argue just because we love the drama of the tension. So, it really is our responsibility to get on the same page with these intense emotions, so that we can live in a more integrated space with them. We need to look at ourselves deep down and say, "Pick an area of your life where you feel dissatisfied. Now, what are you getting out of it?"

One of the more common issues I see with clients who emotionally eat is the theme of lack mentality. While lack-mentality can show up because we enjoy feeling anxious, helpless, or small—it can also show up because we don't want to receive. Women who struggle with receiving often have trouble indulging in delicious food. They don't feel that they deserve to feel good, so they deprive themselves of pleasure. This leads to a myriad of reckless behaviors—like binge eating fast food at all hours of the night, because they are fulfilling a shadow belief.

Breaking down these beliefs has become one of my major practices. I start with a simple list of questions:

1. What is the source of this belief?

2. Where did this belief come from?

3. What behaviors keep perpetuating it?

4. What are some practical tools I can use to address this issue?

5. Am I blaming someone else for this issue?

6. How can I take healthy responsibility for my subconscious beliefs regarding this issue?

As we work through these beliefs, I'm very intentional about walking my client through choosing remedies that feel both *positive* and also *true*. We can't integrate the shadow by faking positivity. It can only be through genuine, compassionate friendship with ourselves that we begin to shift our subconscious beliefs.

Osho, a mystic and philosopher said "Positive thinking is simply the philosophy of hypocrisy, to give it the right name when you're feeling like crying, it teaches you to sing. You can manage if you try but those repressed tears will come out at some point in some situation. There is a limitation to suppression, and the song that you were singing was meaningless. You were not feeling it, it was not born out of your heart."[18]

---

18   Osho. "From Ignorance to Innocence 29." From the series of 30 discourses—Lao Tzu Grove, December 28, 1984. https://oshoworld.com/from-ignorance-to-in-nocence-29/.

Our goal is to become friends with every aspect of ourselves—even the parts of ourselves that other people don't care for—no matter how tumultuous, no matter how wild. And some of this means making space for our sadness.

As uncomfortable as it is, we've got to make time to cry in the shower. To say *Okay, I have twenty minutes on this drive by myself. I'm not calling my mom. I'm going to turn on some sad music and cry. I'm going to grieve—even if I don't know why!* I don't have to name the reason for it to be valid. Tears are important. Being the friend that holds space for our own pain is important. Allowing ourselves to punch pillows, or do kickboxing, or take a rage run is imperative to BE-Friending our anger.

Most of my healing has just been facing disappointments with the mantra, *Okay—I'm going to let this irritating setback help me grieve, heal, and grow.* It can be as insignificant as that idiot who cuts you off on the interstate. Deciding that you're going to use that anger outburst as a way to process unhealed grief is the door to healing.

Finally, sometimes our Shadow is there to keep us safe from pain. Take one of my more recent clients for example—her name was Ellie. Ellie was avoiding rejection by using her body to take up space as a defense mechanism. She said, "I really want to be loved, but I am only going to call my partner in once I have lost the 'extra' weight."

In reality, Ellie thrived at warding people off—even when her weight was a nonissue with them. We discovered Ellie felt more comfortable controlling her rejection. She used her body as a shield to keep others from hurting her. It became armor that protected Ellie from the vulnerability of a meaningful relationship.

By staying in rejection, she didn't have to open herself up. She didn't have to shed the literal and metaphorical layers that kept others out. For Ellie, being authentic felt impossible . . . because letting other people see us is very, very scary.

By maintaining a higher weight than was natural to her body—Ellie was, in every sense of the word, protected. Sadly, she believed it kept her less interesting. It kept her cocooned in a way. Until we started doing the hard work of embracing Shadow Ellie—who we both found to be profoundly lovable, with and without her armor. It is important to note that this was Ellie's unique experience. This is not the case for all larger-bodied people. There is nothing wrong with their size, and they are not using their body as armor. This belief stems from deep fat-phobia and is not helpful for anyone.

So, this is how we BE-Friend ourselves; this integration is how we heal. As we learn to love our hidden parts, the places in us we are afraid to acknowledge, we illuminate them with love and compassion. Shame is welcome here. Jealousy is welcome here. Temptation is welcome here. Confusion is welcome here. Anger is welcome here. Our shadowy parts are welcome here.

All the "sticky" behaviors will be wholly embraced in this space because they deserve to be understood and experienced. As we become better friends to ourselves, we can learn to take a long look at the entirety of our shadows in the mirror and say "Okay, I recognize this uncomfortable truth about myself. It scares me, but I accept it." In turn, we find there is a whole other side to ourselves to discover—that is longing to BE-Friend us too.

20

Be Intimate

"Oh God, help me to believe the truth about myself,
no matter how beautiful it is. Amen."
– *Macrina Wiederkehr, Benedictine Nun*

There is no better feeling than when my man is on top of me. I love the way his body feels against mine. He is amazing—sensitive too! He touches me just right. I remember the first time he touched me *like that*. It overwhelmed my senses . . . until my attention shifted:

Oh God . . . is he touching my—no! Not my butt! Don't grab that, it's huge! Why is he resting his hand on my belly? Don't play with my roll! Oh my God! I'm fat. Will he eventually leave me for a woman hotter than me? He can't be enjoying this . . .

And just like that—I certainly wasn't enjoying anything at all. I'd lost the feeling of being in the moment. Our lovemaking evolved into yet another excuse for me to criticize myself—which in turn pushed him away, leaving me to feel guilty on top of everything else.

Sound familiar?

Too many people rob themselves of intimacy due to insecurities about their appearance, never fully embracing that they are worthy of pleasure regardless of their body size. When we can't relax into the moment because we are obsessing about our perceived flaws, we distance ourselves physically and emotionally from our loving partners. *In turn, we can no longer honor ourselves as sensual beings. Negative talk pushes through and claims everything until nothing is left for us to enjoy.*

Sex can be powerfully liberating or entirely destructive, depending on the relationship we have with ourselves. Sensuality is directly tied to our identity and perceived worth in romantic relationships. Understanding our presence as sensual goddesses is integral to maintaining a loving friendship with ourselves and drowning out the shame-based messages that have followed us since childhood. Attuning to and owning my sexual, feminine energy was a significant piece in healing my poor body image and pressures I felt when I was young. I wanted to maintain my *good-girl* image. This was due in part to my religious upbringing—but society also played a major role in these beliefs.

Inevitably, women disconnect from their most powerful, present energy. They compromise their sanity by calorie counting, and overexercising—which only further presses their sexuality down. They seek pleasure in how their body looks over how it feels. When it comes time to be lavished, or spoiled, they can't receive. It took me a long time to learn how to receive, because *my butt was just too big to enjoy myself* . . .

My husband loves my belly. He finds it sexy. He adores my butt— that's why he touches it. It's been an ongoing conversation throughout our relationship that adds to the work I'm continually doing to adore every part of myself.

In the early stages of dating Olaf, I was enthralled and quite nervous about how he experienced my body. He'd ask to leave the lights on, and I would nervously indulge him. He has always been built, with sculpted muscles and a trim, gorgeous frame. In turn, I was plagued by the thought I was not thin enough for him—until one evening stroll around Santa Monica encouraged me to believe him when he told me what he likes.

As we strolled through the downtown square beneath the full moon, Olaf put his arm around my waist. His hand momentarily hovered over my ribs before he finally said, "Oh, that feels so soft and nice, you didn't have that there before!"

Wait. What? I thought. *Are you freaking kidding me? Did he just tell me I've gained weight?* My thoughts began to race as this gorgeous man continued to compliment something *he liked* about my body. My brain was hellbent on receiving it as an insult.

I couldn't breathe, and my mind was swirling; the conversation stayed with me for days. The concept was difficult to process for years; even now, I don't always take him at his word. I truly believed that *all men like skinny women.* Especially men who are in shape, like Olaf. I had a hard time accepting his enjoyment of my body because I wasn't lavishing myself with my own pleasure and self-acceptance.

To this day, when Olaf touches my booty or my belly in or outside of the bedroom—I remember Santa Monica. I resist the temptation to be insecure and instead celebrate the delicious romance I have with Olaf *and* myself. I meditate on the belief that I am worthy of pleasure, and I am liberated to enjoy it.

Enjoying it can be challenging.

When I work with clients on leaning into their sensuality, many say they haven't had liberating sex in ages and feel closed off sexually. *I encourage them by detailing the many ways to explore self-love and invite pleasure back into their lives.*

My journey of exploring and healing my sexuality was through my study of Tantra.

Tantra is a spiritual path that cultivates love and pleasure to achieve union with the divine. Through this discipline, I learned how to listen to the divine inside my body. It was uncomfortable to feel myself due to years of disconnection; however, I had a guide that led me.

I am not going to pretend that tapping into pleasure is all fun and games. It takes persistence to let go of the blocks and tension that keep pain in place. The fire of Tantra and allowing pleasure is intense. Having someone to support you throughout the process can be the key to true healing. Luckily, I had Dawn Cartwright. Dawn *is* Tantra. Loving. Fierce. Unwavering. Soft. Powerful. Sensitive. She held me when my fear of letting go was intense. She guided me through her wisdom, practices, and witnessing her life.

As I write this, I cannot help but laugh because I was dissatisfied with what my body looked like, but that had little to do with how my body made me feel. Through the presence of breath, movement, and connection, the rigidness of shame softened, and my sexuality came alive. I was then able to connect to how my body felt within myself and in moments of intimacy with my partner.

Through my new practice, pleasure became my guide. I acknowledged my own early sexual trauma and let go of the stories that I was in any way to blame for my negative experiences.

For years, I didn't take my experiences seriously. I thought so many people have awful sexual trauma that mine felt like something I should just get over. After all, it was an 'innocent' experience of a neighbor boy being inappropriate. But after years in NYC receiving catcalls and feeling like I was constantly being violated every time I left the house, I knew there was something more profound to explore. I knew that my six-year-old self was feeling panicked and scared. I had to address this.

And so, gently, with compassion and tons of support, I unwound the contractions in my body, the fear in my heart, and the anger that pulsed through me. The healing that I experienced was intentionally slow. I learned how these experiences of sexual trauma deserve space and a professional who can hold this vulnerability with care.

I had to become intimate and heal my inner best friend before she would be willing to open up to someone else.

When we begin to heal our places of pain, we free ourselves up to be tantalized by our partner's gaze, to have a mind-blowing orgasm that is not eclipsed by fears about the size of our butt. We are present in our pleasure body. Sensuality flows through us—giving us breath and openness. We aren't *tense*, and this is important! Eliminating the tension is everything. I offer the following practice of *Releasing* to my clients—though seemingly small, it can have tremendous benefits. The first part of *Releasing* is as follows:

Create a safe space for yourself.

Pull your body in with your shoulders up and your legs crossed as tightly as possible.

Hold this pose.

Notice what happens to your breath.

Be aware of the sensations in your body and where your mind goes.

Now, imagine walking around like this.

Constricting, isn't it?!

Most of us move through the world unconsciously tensing our body and holding our breath. Sexuality won't thrive in a body that is cramped up—physically, or psychologically.

For me, body shame created a major tension in my body that influenced me to leave the room mentally any time my clothes were off. I'd escape and think about my to-do list, what I was going to order at dinner, or what I could do to make myself more attractive for future moments of intimacy. It was distracting to say the least. After experiencing the second part of *Releasing*, I learned how sexual moments with my partner could feel. Try it—and imagine the possibility of this new way of *being* in the bedroom:

Uncross your legs.

Open your chest.

Take a deep breath.

Move your shoulders up and down.

Breathe into your body.

Close your eyes and visualize yourself walking around holding the openness in your body.

Imagine yourself walking down the street feeling alive in your sex center—fully feeling and owning your sexuality.

What does it feel like? Is it scary? Liberating? Can you imagine walking around in the world embodied? How would that make you feel? How would that change your relationships?

The caveat here is to acknowledge if you *don't* feel safe and to believe me when I say *That is completely okay!* Throughout my work, I have observed a direct correlation between sexual trauma and eating disorders. If you're struggling with both sexual and food issues, and this exercise leaves your body feeling uncomfortable—be gentle with yourself! You might not be ready. If this unearths trauma, that is common, and it is important to pace yourself or reach out to a coach, counselor, or therapist if you need it! The goal of this exercise is to BE-Friend ourselves, but sometimes this can be disarming. Healing will happen as your body learns to feel safe; the more we treat ourselves with compassion, the safer we feel!

There is nothing more beautiful than a confident, embodied woman. It doesn't even matter what she looks like. True to her core, when she walks into the room everyone is enamored—she is vibrant, radiant, and sexy. It has nothing to do with her weight; it has everything to do with her magnitude. This type of self-sovereignty cannot be faked. Trust me, I've tried. There is no substitute for showing up as the whole, fleshy, gorgeous goddesses we are and receiving the pleasure that is rightfully ours for the taking. We deserve to feel good; we deserve a full helping of delicious pleasure.

The whimsical ways of intimacy are mystical and unpredictable. It leads us into the deepest places of ourselves and beckons us back into our bodies. It challenges our beliefs and requires us to consider the negative messages we've been receiving about our appearance since birth. It invites the past to unearth itself and creates room for healing and inner compassion. Exploring the depths of our own sensuality is yet another way we can be an excellent friend to ourselves. Friends have fun together; they set us free to indulge—we learn to enjoy the world better when we explore our body in new ways.

Pleasure is not limited to sexual expression and experience. It includes all kinds of indulgences: delighting in food, indulging in relaxation, exploring new hobbies, and investing in self-care. It all melds together and influences the way we nourish our physical form, spirits, and souls. As we use our senses to explore life, we experience an unfolding romance. It's in everything—wrapping up in a cozy blanket, sipping a delicious glass of wine, smelling freshly picked flowers from the garden.

It's intimate! Especially our relationship with food that engages every part of us and makes us *feel* things.

I mean, I don't know about you, but I've certainly seen slices of coconut creme pie, strawberry cheesecake topped extravagantly with a red berry and delicious crumbles, and svelte pieces of double chocolate cake that *are so sexy*! *What a dish*—that would involve my sight, smell, taste, and touch to enjoy it; to delight in its flavor, weight, and texture. *When I allow myself to delight in it*, food can be a sensual experience.

The trouble is, I haven't always allowed myself permission to enjoy food. Instead, I've eyeballed the glamorous cake tiers at parties, then been thrust into a panicked state of hypervigilance, wild sweating, and calorie counting. In those situations, by the time I'm eating the cake, I'm shoveling—not tasting; then, I find myself going in for a second *shame slice*, even if my stomach is full. *Not exactly what I'd call a pleasureful experience!*

What I've learned is that the way we engage food and sex can be parallel, and in many cases, one becomes a substitute for the other, and the binge-purge cycle that shows up in one space presents in the other. Take my work with Libby for example:

Libby was a very creative and sensual woman. As we dove into our work together, she shared how, as a preteen, her father caught her kissing a boy behind a shed. One of the most exciting and freeing moments of her development was exposed and condemned. For her father, Libby kissing boys represented a loss of paternal control. He was terrified. From that moment on, Libby's mom and dad treated her like she was promiscuous. They ruled the home with fear. Not only did they ground her for *the incident*, but they made sure any possibility of Libby experiencing pleasure was squashed. Her sensuality and sexual expression were defined as *bad* and *wrong*, that she needed to *watch out* and *behave*!

As an adult, guess where Libby began to work out these frustrations? You guessed it: *With food!* Food was pleasure, and pleasures were bad. In turn, she would control and obsess with every binge. Bread was bad; sweets were devilish. So, she couldn't eat them in the open—only behind closed doors—fast and quick, so no one would find out.

Most of us who struggle with food think that food is the culprit, but I've rarely seen that to be the case. Food is the top layer of a very deep issue or toxic belief. Once we uncover the root issue, food itself often takes a back seat.

When we restrict and starve ourselves in either area, or paint our needs and cravings as *bad*, we are more likely to end up creating the issues we've been trying to avoid, including emotional eating, weight gain, and a myriad of physical symptoms. Don't we deserve better? Don't we deserve to feel excellent inside ourselves? I think so.

Consider this chapter the enlivening call to *take your body back*! The sexy, magnificent, woman you are is dying to be intimate. So, indulge it! Be spicy, be erotic, be enlivened, and naughty … *with yourself!* I cannot emphasize the importance of self-pleasuring enough. Experiment. Play. Enjoy. When we are sexual with other people, there are inherent boundaries to uphold to preserve ourselves. Without self-exploration, we rob ourselves of the opportunity to learn our own strengths and boundaries. Pleasing ourselves helps create a safe space to be with ourselves *for ourselves*—something that is truly profound.

Yes, it might be triggering, so be encouraged. Take your time. Take it easy. Go slow. Explore all the parts of yourself. Be soft. I teach my clients that we are like houses with several stories of brilliant rooms. Embark on self-exploration as though you are unlocking new internal rooms that have yet to be discovered.

Yes, it will be emotional.

Yes, it might take practice.

But it will be expansive above all things and a cause for self-celebration. The more you are intimate with yourself, the more you will reclaim your body and be able to show up in the world as the vibrant, passionate, mystical goddess you were created to be—*finally*!

21

Be Celebratory

My appetite has always been voracious—for food, for pleasure, for life. I was born that way, I guess. I was always the girl who could eat the most. I loved indulging. When I was little, I'd get swept away by the enchantment of birthday parties. It was the whimsicality of them—the colors, the sweet smells, the sound of play and laughter. Naturally, there was the snack table, which I always gravitated toward. I'd approach trays of delicious treats and treat myself to one of the best parts of living. I'd allow my belly to expand in my floral sundress, to relax my body beneath the bright sky and not worry about how it compared to the others surrounding me.

Prior to learning indulgence was *wrong*, I allowed myself to feel excitement about everything—which invited a sense of play, presence, and delight children cultivate naturally. As adults, we have trouble with ease—save the few and far moments in between where it chooses us . . . to gently remind us how to *be*.

I remember one easy memory on the beach that still feels like a dream every time I think of it. I was with my niece, and we were splashing in the clear, blue waves—our skin covered in sun, with sand upon our faces; then Kiki looked up, smiled widely, and said, "Oh my gosh, Aunt Mar! Your butt looks so big in that bikini! It looks great!"

Initially, her comment made me lose my breath. But her vivacious splashing and playful eyebrow raise made it clear she had meant it as a compliment. My internal response made our differences evident—we were from an entirely different generation.

As a child of the 2000s, she was raised to celebrate *the booty*, whereas I was raised in an era where having a *big butt* was a major issue. Shrinking your assets meant stocking your pantry with powders, shakes, and all things nonfat. Because *fat* was wrong . . . especially in the back.

I suppose we can thank the Kardashians for shifting our societal appreciation for great behinds. They certainly shook me awake and challenged my belief that *the smaller I am, the better I'll look*. This embrace supplemented the compassion I was already giving to my thick, muscular, athletic butt. So . . . *big*? For some, they would laugh at this notion—because these things are all a matter of perspective. Still, I can relish in the idea—to me, on my body—*it is* big. And since that day, I've come to embrace a compliment I wouldn't have been able to receive twenty years ago.

Kiki's right . . . what's not to love? My husband loves my butt . . . he compliments it all the time. Olaf agrees that I could gain weight and he'd gladly enjoy it . . . *because it gives him more flesh to hold onto*. But most importantly, it is how I feel about ME. So, I applaud the notion that butts, bellies, boobs, hips, and thighs should be celebrated at every size.

While I am still learning, I have now experienced ease around my appetite. I've released my shame around the great unifiers—food, sex, pleasure, indulgence, and release. And my relaxation into these things is how I BE-Friend myself. I no longer weaponize the things that make me feel full, alive, sensual, and present.

I'm still a work-in-process myself, just like you. It's okay to stumble and fall along the way. What truly matters is that we pick ourselves up and keep leaning into love as we continue to learn and grow.

Teaching other people to do the same has empowered us both and expanded our lives. My life's work is breathing love into others so that they too can learn how to *BE-Friend themselves*.

That is my hope for you, Dear Reader—May compassion, light, and love lead the way.

Please remember to celebrate yourself, and know that I am celebrating you too on this incredible journey of self-discovery and self-acceptance. Your path is an inspiration to us all.

Acknowledgments

Gratitude is the ultimate state of receiving.
– Dr. Joe Dispenza

This book came to life because I was open to receiving support and love from the incredible people in my life. It stands as a testament to the countless blessings I've experienced.

Throughout this process, I've been enriched by the presence of those who offered emotional cheerleading, writing expertise, book editing, and marketing know-how. Their guiding hands have made all the difference.

First and foremost, I want to express my heartfelt gratitude to Olaf and Aspen. You both have been my rocks, creating a nurturing space for this creative endeavor. Your unwavering love, encouragement, and genuine care for my well-being have propelled me forward.

A special mention goes to Jonathan Barbato and Cari Schaefer, who lovingly pushed me to dive into this project. Jonathan, your infectious excitement gave me the boost I needed when I had no idea where to begin. You both have been open doors for questions, edits, collaborative ideas, and friendship.

Autumn Jade Monrow, your guidance, humor, and enlightened words have made writing an enjoyable experience for me. Our work together wove a beautiful tapestry of healing, friendship, and connection.

I appreciate your reflections and the way you cared for my message.

To the brilliant minds of Sharon Brock, Kim Chestney, Kara Masters, Jacob Liberman, Michael Hoffman, Junie Moon, Tom Owen, Katie Hoffman and Shelley Sage Heart, I am grateful for your understanding of the creative process and the loving support you've provided.

I want to extend my appreciation to the amazing women who kept my vibe high, allowed pleasure to flow, and taught me to embrace my truth: Arriane Alexander, Amanda Young, Eva Clay, and A'magine Nation.

A heartfelt thank you goes out to my mentors, coaches, and healers: Dr. Norwood Yamini, Dawn Cartwright, Amber Krys, Lara Catone, Olaf Hartmann, Carmen Larino, and Sarah Sol.

Suzanne, you have been my biggest cheerleader, providing a safe space for me to share my story and offering endless hours of edits and revisions.

Mom, Dad, and Jill, your excitement and constant support have meant the world to me.

To my clients who trusted me with the depths of their hearts, thank you. Your presence in my journey has been transformative, and I honor you for allowing me to hold space for your healing.

Finally, God, what a ride it has been! Your constant presence and endless surprises never cease to amaze me. Thank you for everything.

THE END

More
BE-Friending Yourself
Resources

Download the Body-Love Meditation at
https://www.loveyourbodyloveyourself.com/body-love

Receive the Free "Breaking the Cycle of Emotional Eating"
Video Course
https://goloveyourbodyloveyourself.com/emotionaleating

Participate in exclusive live videos, material, and resources at
**https://www.facebook.com/groups/
peacewithfoodandbodyconfidence**

Watch more by Marla Mervis-Hartmann at
**https://www.instagram.com/loveyourbodyloveyourselfalways/
https://www.youtube.com/marlamervis**

Printed in the USA
CPSIA information can be obtained
at www.ICGtesting.com
CBHW041932151024
15908CB00046B/1032